THE CHRISTIAN COUNSELING
A Guide to Healing T

HOPE & HEALING FOR GRIEF

WRITTEN BY
KEVIN ELLERS, D.MIN.

Copyright © 2023 by Kevin Ellers

ALL RIGHTS RESERVED

No part of this book may be reproduced, stored in a retrieval system, or transmitted in any form or by any means—electronic, mechanical, photocopy, recording, or otherwise—without prior written permission of the copyright owner, except brief quotations used in connection with reviews in magazines or newspapers.

Unless otherwise noted, all passages of Scripture are from THE HOLY BIBLE, NEW INTERNATIONAL VERSION®, NIV® Copyright © 1973, 1978, 1984, 2011 by Biblica, Inc.® Used by permission. All rights reserved worldwide.

Scripture quotations marked AMP are taken from the Amplified Bible, Copyright © 2015 by The Lockman Foundation, La Habra, CA 90631. All rights reserved.

Scripture quotations marked ISV are taken from the International Standard Version, Copyright © 1995—2014 by ISV Foundation. ALL RIGHTS RESERVED INTERNATIONALLY. Used by permission of Davidson Press, LLC.

Scripture quotations marked ESV are taken from the Holy Bible, English Standard Version. ESV® Text Edition: 2016. Copyright © 2001 by Crossway Bibles, a publishing ministry of Good News Publishers.

Cover design by Trenton Haddock

Interior design by Anne McLaughlin, Blue Lake Design

ISBN: 978-1-960624-03-1

Published by AACC Publishing, Forest, Virginia

Printed in the United States

Publisher's note: This workbook is not intended to be a substitute for professional help. It is designed to provide information, personal insights, and a path forward toward hope and healing. For diagnosis or treatment of any mental health problem, consult your physician, licensed therapist, psychiatrist, or other trained professional. Neither the author nor the AACC shall be liable for any physical, psychological, emotional, financial, or commercial damages, including but not limited to special, incidental, consequential, or other damages. Mental health conditions are complex and best evaluated by a physical examination and consultation with a qualified clinician, with an agreed-upon personalized treatmen plan to follow.

Dear Friend,

Our team developed this *Hope & Healing* workbook series for those who are struggling with nagging emotional pain, a crushing sense of loss, and/or mental health challenges in their everyday lives and want to bring God into the equation as they look forward to a better future. We've chosen these topics because people have told us they need resources to deal with these complex and difficult problems.

This series is also designed for our members—counselors, coaches, chaplains, pastors, and others—to complement and increase their effectiveness in care and counseling ministry.

Featuring some of the world's leading experts, each subject is based on the latest research and best practices, overflows with the love and grace of God, and is anchored in His Word. In short, these workbooks provide roadmaps that are clinically excellent and distinctively Christian.

We pray that God will set your feet on a path to new life, and you will be deeply encouraged by the wisdom, compassion, and care flowing from each page.

We can't wait for you to start, and we look forward to hearing how God works in and through you. Our hope is in Him.

> Now to him who is able to do far more abundantly than all that we ask or think, according to the power at work within us, to him be glory in the church and in Christ Jesus throughout all generations, forever and ever. Amen. (Ephesians 3:20-21 ESV)

God be with you. We love being a part of your life.

Sincerely,

Dr. Tim Clinton
President
American Association of Christian Counselors

Contents

Introduction		7
Chapter 1	What Is Grief?	11
Chapter 2	What Are My Losses?	25
Chapter 3	Grief and Personality	41
Chapter 4	Support Systems During Grief	49
Chapter 5	Strategic Grieving: Mourning Rituals, Ceremonies, and Activities	57
Chapter 6	Forward Movement and Continuing Bonds	73
Chapter 7	When It Doesn't Get Better	81
Chapter 8	So Now What?: Spiritual Dimensions of Grief	99
Appendix	Bible Passages for Those Who Grieve	117
Endnotes		121
About the Author		123
About the AACC		124
Resources		128

INTRODUCTION

Though the Lord gives you the bread of adversity and the water of oppression, yet your Teacher will no longer hide Himself, but your eyes will [constantly] see your Teacher.

ISAIAH 30:20 AMP

"Time heals all wounds."

No doubt you've heard this old adage, but do you believe it to be true? I used to agree that time is a great healer. I still believe it *can* be, but that's not always the case. I've discovered in my research and years of experience that healing results not from time alone; it's what we do during that time that makes a difference.

If you're reading this workbook, it is probably because you have experienced loss or are trying to help someone who is grieving. Whatever your situation, I'm sorry that you are dealing with pain and sorrow. It hurts when you experience a loss, and often, it hurts even worse to watch someone you love undergoing a painful experience. It's common to feel helpless in the face of someone else's pain and grief—especially if you don't how to respond or what to do.

This workbook is birthed from countless hours of working with grievers over thirty years. From my initial experiences of helping people through trauma and loss, I became intrigued by how differently people respond in the aftermath of trauma and loss. I wanted to discover why some people not only survived, but often demonstrated significant emotional, spiritual, and relational growth. I now have a better understanding of what those people do that sets them apart from others who can't seem to shake their grief, and who may even have adverse long-term impacts.

Seasons of Grief

For many years, I've opened my grief workshops and classes with the following question: "Do you know what the death rate is in your state?" The obvious answer is 100 percent, but we don't like to think about that. Unless Jesus returns soon, I will die, you will die, your family and friends will die, and your pets will die. It's not possible to avoid death in our world. We don't like it, it's painful, and most of us would rather not have to deal with losing those we love or facing our own death.

Depressing? It *can* be, yet if you *acknowledge* this truth, it should remind you that everyone has periods of grief in their lives; you are not alone. And if you're able to *embrace* this fact, it can help you begin to see life very differently and prompt you to live a life of full engagement.

I don't want to sugarcoat the excruciating pain of grief. It can sometimes be so intense, overwhelming, and confusing that you aren't sure you can make it through another day. You may experience a vacillating kaleidoscope of emotions that threaten to overwhelm you. Or you may feel numb, detached, and as if you're in a bad dream. Both responses are normal, but at some point, you must face the truth to heal and grow. To learn life's most important lessons, we need to wade into the deep end of the proverbial grief pool.

In my work with grieving people, we frequently talk about the importance of "forward movement" in grief. I caution them to avoid trying to force their experience into stages because *every person is different, every loss is distinct, and every circumstance is unique*. I do, however, tend to view grief in three seasons: impact, confronting, and rebuilding through the process of meaning-making. This workbook will focus on practical aspects in each of these seasons with exercises designed to help you experience genuine growth and transformation.

Grief can make it hard to concentrate. It impacts short-term memory, often making it difficult to process complex concepts. Therefore, I haven't written this workbook from an academic perspective. I'll be using simple language, but that doesn't mean the content is superficial. It comes from the wisdom of grievers.

This workbook is an invitation—indeed, a plea—to step out of the natural and normal tendency to deny the reality of pain and suffering. Until you admit and address your grief, you won't grow. You'll remain stagnant. I truly believe that even in the midst of your pain, you, like many others I have accompanied through their grief, can do much more than just survive. You can thrive through the experience, learn more about yourself, and even find a new sense of mission in this life. As you do, you'll discover that this path through pain is the way to become increasingly transformed into the image of the God who loves you.

You can't "fix" grief. Instead, this book will help guide you through your grief. The exercises are important because they will help lead you to growth and emotional and spiritual wellness. They can help you understand grief and will provide practical tools to grow emotionally and spiritually from your loss. This grief workbook is a practical companion to my more in-depth book and curriculum, *The Grief Factor,* and focuses primarily on eight core concepts of grief.

Healthy Response to Grief

As you work through the content, reflective questions, and exercises in this book, some of the goals will be to achieve healthy response to grief. Several responses are common among the healthiest grievers, including:

> Facing their loss and confronting their denial

> An openness and acceptance of their emotions, thoughts, and struggles

> Active engagement in confronting their grief without comparing themselves to others

> A sense of self-compassion and the realization they can't recover on their own

> Surrendering their loss to God

> Shifting from asking "Why?" questions to "What now?"

> Taking responsibility for their own grief and growth in their journey

> Ability to reposition after a loss and learn to explore new interests

> Seeking out healing and fulfilling relationships

> Reevaluating their life and redefining a new sense of mission and purpose

I want to be real with you about two things. First, as you face your grief it will require you to embrace your pain…and it will hurt. But, second, if you work your way through these exercises, you can come out the other side wiser, stronger, and more compassionate than you ever imagined.

My prayer for you is that you will not just survive your loss, but that this journey will help you develop a better understanding of yourself, as well as a greater appreciation for life and those you love. Grief is a wake-up call for many people. It has often changed the priorities, relationships, and trajectory of their lives. I hope that during this journey you will discover the amazing person God has created you to be and that as you wrestle through different facets of your grief you will discover a joy and a peace that truly passes all understanding.

CHAPTER 1
WHAT IS GRIEF?

Grief Discovery

Healthy grievers have an awareness and understanding of grief and its impact on their lives.

From time to time, we all suffer profound sadness after losing something precious to us. It may be the loss of a family member, a divorce or relational breakup, the death of a dream, the rejection of a friend, or a tragic medical diagnosis threatening loss of health. Something in our core has shifted—like an earthquake sending off shock waves and knocking us off balance.

One of my favorite scriptures is Psalm 42 (printed below). It describes the hurt, longing, and hard questions we ask when we suffer loss. As we begin this study, I want us to pause to explore the powerful emotions expressed by the writer. Take some time to read through this psalm several times. Reflect on words or phrases that capture your attention. I encourage you to sit with each line and write notes beside it that surface during your meditation. You may relate strongly to a word or verse. Don't analyze your reaction—simply let it flow. You may find it interesting to return to this journaling months or years from now and see significant shifts in your head and heart relating to your loss.

Psalm 42

[1] As the deer pants for streams of water,
    so my soul pants for you, my God.
[2] My soul thirsts for God, for the living God.
    When can I go and meet with God?
[3] My tears have been my food
    day and night,

    while people say to me all day long,
        "Where is your God?"
4 These things I remember
    as I pour out my soul:
    how I used to go to the house of God
    under the protection of the Mighty One
    with shouts of joy and praise
    among the festive throng.
5 Why, my soul, are you downcast?
    Why so disturbed within me?
    Put your hope in God,
    for I will yet praise him,
    my Savior and my God.
6 My soul is downcast within me;
    therefore I will remember you
    from the land of the Jordan,
    the heights of Hermon—from Mount Mizar.
7 Deep calls to deep
    in the roar of your waterfalls;
    all your waves and breakers
    have swept over me.
8 By day the Lord directs his love,
    at night his song is with me—
    a prayer to the God of my life.
9 I say to God my Rock,
    "Why have you forgotten me?
    Why must I go about mourning,
    oppressed by the enemy?"
10 My bones suffer mortal agony
    as my foes taunt me,
    saying to me all day long,
    "Where is your God?"

[11] Why, my soul, are you downcast?
    Why so disturbed within me?
    Put your hope in God,
    for I will yet praise him,
    my Savior and my God.

What Does Grief Look Like?

People use the word "grief" in many ways to describe a lot of different experiences. Regardless of the word we use, it's important to understand the various components of grief. Let's look at several examples and then some other words closely associated with loss and grief.

> Joe is a 78-year-old man whose wife died six months ago from a sudden heart attack after 50 years of marriage. He owns his business, and after taking two days off, he went back to work and started staying late. He has seen no decline in his ability to perform at work. His children are concerned because they say he hasn't dealt with his wife's death. They haven't seen him cry, even at the funeral. He was previously very healthy, but over the past six months, he has had numerous physical illnesses and very low energy. Other than working, he hasn't done any of the things he used to enjoy, like fishing and gardening.

> Sara is a 50-year-old woman whose husband died in a car accident. She has been almost incapacitated in the six months since his death. She is still, in her words, "just a big baby and crying all the time." She doesn't feel her friends are sensitive to her overwhelming loss, but then, she too struggles with the belief that she should be able to "snap out of it" and "return to normal." She has continued to work. Her boss has been patient with her, but she's afraid she's going to be fired.

> John is a 65-year-old top executive whose company was bought out after many years. The new owners called him in one day and said they were going in a new direction. He was close to retirement, so they gave him a very generous severance package and lots of accolades, and they honored him for his many years of service. He came out financially better than if he had stayed until retirement. Still, six

months later, John is severely depressed and suicidal. His family is confused and doesn't understand what the issue is.

Mary was happily married for 45 years. Her husband died three months ago of cancer after two long, hard years of suffering, but she appears to be doing very well and seems very much at peace. Her children think she's in denial about his death because they can't tell that she has shown any signs of grief. They question if she's just stuffing her emotions and not dealing with her husband's death, or as one daughter asked, "Did she really even love dad? It doesn't seem like it." Most people assume she can't be doing as well as she appears, that maybe she is just putting on a face for others.

As you examine these four examples, ask yourself: What are the losses? Who is grieving? What is the right way to grieve?

Actually, all four people are grieving in their own way, but grief can look very different to the outside world. We need to learn the language of grief and distinguish between the *felt experiences* of grief and the *processes* of mourning. Most people associate grief with death. However, some losses can be even greater than a death. Let's look at some terms.

Bereavement

Bereavement is a term commonly used after someone has died. For example, society would consider a woman to be bereaved after the death of her husband. This is true regardless of the health of their relationship or any of the circumstances around the death. Objectively, her husband has died, and she is the bereaved widow.

Yet the root of the word *bereavement* carries the connotation of having something taken away by force—of losing or being robbed of something. Friends would say of the widow that she "lost her husband." The interesting thing about this, however, is that we aren't able to investigate her heart and mind, so we don't know if or how she considers herself to be bereaved. So basically, bereavement is about what you have lost.

This topic came up during a grief class I was teaching. A man raised his hand and said, "I can appreciate this discussion. When my father died, I remember thinking, *I'm glad the SOB is dead. He was a horrible human being, and the world truly is a better place without him in it!* I know that sounds harsh, but unfortunately, it's reality." Several people in the class nodded in agreement as they thought about other specific people who had died.

Let me give you another example: Suzie was married to a police officer for 40 years, but he had been killed in the line of duty six months previously. He was tough, strict, and not very affectionate. Those characteristics were an asset at work where he was known as a no-nonsense, hardworking cop and had a long record of outstanding performance. In a marriage, however, those same traits created fear and distance. When he came home each day, he brought his fierce demeanor and protective walls with him. He had very little connection with Suzie or their children, who at the time of his death were grown and living hundreds of miles away. She had considered divorcing him, but didn't feel the church would condone this decision. She had been taught to submit to his authority as the head of the house. Few people were aware that Suzie and her husband had such a difficult relationship. For decades, she had isolated from others and was able to hide it.

At his funeral, Suzie struggled with the perception of him everyone—except her—shared. As I processed his death with her, I saw that she struggled most with feelings of guilt—not anger or sorrow. Secretly, his death brought Suzie a sense of relief. He had taken good care of the family financially, so she didn't have to worry about security. She was more concerned about losing her relationships with the other cops' spouses. She wondered if she would still be included in their get-togethers. She was bereaved, but did she feel the loss in the way others thought she did? No, not at all. Were there secondary losses that she would later face that she was unaware of now? Probably. In these situations, sometimes the grief is less about the loss of a person than about the death of a dream—in this case, a dream of what a marriage could or should have been.

What is Grief?

In some of the exercises in this workbook, we'll look at a wide range of losses people suffer. You may need to make some difficult life adjustments, but you don't *grieve* unless you have lost something. You may have losses which others don't know about, that you keep hidden. You might have others you may not even be aware of for quite some time.

Grief is the most common term used after a loss. Take a moment to write your own definition of the word. (It's important for you to do this now because we'll come back to it later.) Don't try to look it up in a dictionary or on the internet!

My definition of grief is: Dealing w/ the loss of my person and missing him so very much. Grief is the feeling of aloneness and the loss of love from someone who knew me so well. Grief is suffering for the future as I knew it. My whole world has changed. I am lost without him and would be happy to be with him in heaven vs. being left on this earth w/o him.

Do you know how you arrived at this definition or where you learned to grieve? Take some time to reflect on these questions:

1. What is the first loss you remember? Death of my mother and my Aunt Juanita.

2. How and when did you learn how to grieve? I have been suffering for 3½ years from anticipatory grief watching and caring for my husband who suffered from Stage IV terminal cancer and brain radiation necrosis.

3. What did you learn about grief from those around you? Nothing

For many people, the first loss is during childhood. Typically, it is the death of a pet or an older relative. However, some children experience multiple losses early in their lives. I always use this exercise in my grief classes and then have participants discuss their answers with another person or in a small group. Note that in my instructions, I don't ask about the *first death* you experienced. This was intentional. Not all losses involve the death of a person.

Take a few minutes to think through your life. What are some of the losses that you experienced other than someone's physical death? Write them here:

> - Loss of my mom through her severe depression & alcoholism
> - Loss of my childhood because I began to take care of my mom from 6 years old due to my Dad's suicide

When people respond to this question, some of the answers I get are relationships, possessions, status, community, divorce, moving, and innocence. In the next chapter, we will go more in depth by doing a Life Impact Timeline exercise. Later we will explore this even more thoroughly to see how these losses shaped you and the positive or negative lessons you learned. Sometimes you learn that others were there for you and you felt nurtured. Or you may feel that people didn't notice your loss, didn't acknowledge it, minimized it, or denied it even happened. Various traumas and losses may be consciously or unconsciously hidden because of shame or a variety of other reasons.

I often ask group members, "Why do we grieve? Do you have an idea of why you grieve some losses, but not others?" **In short, we grieve after we lose things we love and have formed attachments to.** In the absence of love and attachment, we may experience a variety of emotions, but they don't usually include genuine grief. For example, I watch the news almost every night. Here in Chicago, we are constantly bombarded by instances of violence and murder. While I sometimes feel angry about the situation and feel empathy and compassion for the families, I usually don't feel strong personal feelings of grief. Why? Because I don't know those people intimately. It's sad that they've lost a loved one, but I have no connection to them. However, a police officer may watch another cop die, and even though he doesn't know that individual, he feels a sense of connection and brotherhood that triggers powerful emotions of grief.

Most people's definition of grief centers around the feeling and expression of emotional pain. Grief hurts. Literally! However, I want to expand your definition of grief beyond an emotional state. Grief is all-encompassing. It impacts the cognitive function of the brain as well as our emotions. We can literally feel it in our bodies. Stress may cause muscles in our neck and shoulders to become tense. We may experience things like ulcers or gastrointestinal problems. Emotional pain can result in a compromised immune system and many other physical ailments. Unresolved, unabating, long-term grief can literally kill you.

Common Reactions Experienced After Loss and Trauma

Following a traumatic event, people commonly experience a number of reactions that may seem negative and not feel normal. The impacts of grief on the following lists, though quite varied, are all normal reactions among those undergoing traumatic experiences.[1] Place a checkmark beside any of the effects you have experienced.

Physical Effects

- [x] Fatigue, exhaustion
- [ ] Increased physical pain
- [x] Sleep disturbances
- [x] Cardiovascular strain
- [ ] Reduced immune response
- [x] Decreased appetite
- [ ] Decreased libido
- [ ] Hyperarousal
- [ ] Nausea
- [ ] Dizziness
- [x] Headaches

CHAPTER 1   19

- [x] Gastrointestinal problems
- [ ] Increased startle response
- [ ] Muscle tremors
- [ ] Profuse sweating
- [x] Digestive problems
- [ ] Somatic complaints
- [ ] Ritualistic behavior
- [x] More accident prone

Emotional Effects

- [x] Shock
- [x] Fear/terror
- [x] Irritability
- [ ] Anger
- [x] Grief or sadness
- [x] Depression
- [x] Despair
- [x] Loss of pleasure from familiar activities
- [x] Nervousness
- [ ] Blame
- [x] Guilt
- [x] Emotional Numbing
- [x] Helplessness
- [ ] Identification with the victim
- [x] Difficulty feeling happy

Interpersonal Effects

- [x] Increased relational conflict
- [ ] Reduced relational intimacy
- [x] Impaired work performance
- [ ] Impaired school performance
- [ ] Feeling abandoned/rejected
- [x] Social withdrawal
- [x] Alienation
- [ ] Decreased satisfaction
- [x] Distrust
- [ ] Externalization of blame
- [x] Externalization of vulnerability
- [x] Overprotectiveness

Cognitive Effects

- [x] Impaired concentration
- [x] Impaired decision-making ability
- [x] Memory impairment
- [x] Disbelief
- [ ] Confusion
- [ ] Distortion
- [x] Self-blame
- [x] Decreased self-esteem
- [ ] Decreased self-efficacy
- [x] Worry
- [x] Dissociation (e.g., tunnel vision, dreamlike or "spacey" feeling)

Spiritual Effects

- ☐ Spiritual disconnection with God
- ☑ Questioning God and theological beliefs
- ☐ Anger at God
- ☑ Spiritual emptiness
- ☐ Withdrawal from the faith community
- ☑ Increased awareness of morality
- ☑ Guilt for feelings (i.e. anger, desire for vengeance)

It's not unusual to experience many of these symptoms in the early days of grieving a significant loss. Typically, grievers find that as time goes on, the symptoms lessen in three important areas: frequency, intensity, and duration. However, some people find that they experience some of them more intensely after time has passed.

If it has been some time since your loss, you may want to go back and rank key effects on a scale of 1 to 10, contrasting the impact you felt in the early days after the loss with how you feel today. You will probably find that the frequency, intensity, and duration of your symptoms have diminished. However, it's important to understand that you can expect times when these effects spike. They may be triggered by a date on the calendar, a conversation, a picture, a memory, or the anniversary of the loss. People are sometimes surprised when they feel the impacts have lessened and then find them unexpectedly activated into a higher state, especially at the one- or two-year mark. When that happens, it's important to stop and face the new feeling of pain. It will gradually subside if you don't stuff it. In summary, you experience grief in your head, heart, and body because of a perceived loss.

Mourning

Mourning consists of the things you do after a loss, including the time you take to grieve, rituals in which you may participate, actions you engage in (or avoid) for a while, ways you dress, and how you engage with others. Many people use the words *grieving* and *mourning* interchangeably, which isn't typically a problem, yet I believe it brings greater clarity to think of "mourning" as what you do with the grief you are experiencing.

We can mourn a loss before the death occurs, which is common with prolonged health declines for some forms of cancer and Alzheimer's disease. Grievers are sometimes confused or feel guilt when they feel more relief than sadness after a death. I help them see that they may have already done a lot of mourning in anticipation of the death.

Think about the terms we have discussed so far and answer these questions:

Can you be bereaved and not experience grief? Why or why not?

I guess so?

Can you mourn, but not really experience grief? Why or why not?

?

The answer to both questions is yes. I was teaching this concept in class years ago. A chaplain told of a female firefighter in his firehouse who had recently ended her life by suicide, and the funeral was going to be in a few days. Half of the firefighters couldn't stand her and had very poor relationships with her, but others were very close to her. At the funeral, they all attended because it was expected, but only half of them experienced it as a loss and grieved. The others participated in the mourning ritual by attending and showing respect, but they didn't have a painful sense of loss. They may have been sad, but they were honestly relieved that they wouldn't have to put up with her anymore.

In the next chapter, you will work on your Life Impact Timeline. One of the later exercises will challenge you to go back and assess the significant losses from three dimensions: Was the loss recognized? How you were able or unable to experience grief? And have you truly mourned that loss? Later, I will ask you to consider the next steps in what you need to do to come to terms with the loss and experience grief. It's never too late to grieve! In my coaching practice, we have "divorce funeral rituals"—we bury something, burn something, and create rituals to show something has ended. You can't rebuild a life if you are carrying something dead with you. The stench of death and the weight dragging behind you is a powerful deterrent to healthy relationships.

To live is to be vulnerable. To grieve well and experience growth, we must face our grief. C.S. Lewis explains:

> There is no safe investment. To love at all is to be vulnerable. Love anything, and your heart will certainly be wrung and possibly broken. If you want to make sure of keeping it intact, you must give your heart to no one, not even to an animal. Wrap it carefully round with hobbies and little luxuries; avoid all entanglements; lock it up safe in the casket or coffin of your selfishness. But in that casket—safe, dark, motionlessness, airless—it will change. It will not be broken; it will become unbreakable, impenetrable, irredeemable. The alternative to tragedy, or at least to the risk of tragedy, is damnation. The only place outside of Heaven where you can be perfectly safe from all the dangers and perturbations of love is Hell.[2]
>
> **C.S. LEWIS,** *THE FOUR LOVES*

CHAPTER 2

WHAT ARE MY LOSSES?

Therefore, since we have been justified through faith, we have peace with God through our Lord Jesus Christ, through whom we have gained access by faith into this grace in which we now stand. And we boast in the hope of the glory of God. Not only so, but we also glory in our sufferings, because we know that suffering produces perseverance, perseverance, character; and character, hope. And hope does not put us to shame, because God's love has been poured out into our hearts through the Holy Spirit, who has been given to us.

ROMANS 5:1-5

Grief Discovery

Healthy grievers are aware of their losses and face them.

Many years ago, when I was just getting started as a marriage and family therapist, I went to a marriage seminar where Dr. H. Norman Wright made a statement that has stuck with me to this day. He said that one of the first things you need to do when working with a couple is to help them recognize the unidentified losses they have never dealt with. I have expanded this statement and believe it is critical for all healthy humans to acknowledge their past, particularly if it is still impacting our present. We must face the impact on us, then move forward and focus on growth. You can't change your past, but you don't have to let it negatively define you for the rest of your life. If you get beyond your fear and face it, it no longer has the power to drive you to negative, ineffective, and self-sabotaging behaviors.

When the Past Is Still Present

Whether you're aware of it or not, you have been greatly influenced and shaped by the people and circumstances of your life—and will continue to be. One of the most critical exercises I do with my clients is a Life Impact Timeline. Through the years, I have found that many people seek help only when the pain and discomfort of their life reaches a breaking point. They go to a therapist, pastor, or coach with a presenting problem. However, qualified people helpers often realize that the real problem is not what the person is complaining about. The source is something deeper.

Some are ready to address these deep-rooted issues and grow; others aren't. In order to grow, we must acknowledge the events from our past that have shaped us. Only then can we invite God to help us change them. Until we are aware of their impact, it will be very difficult to address the problems that affect our thinking and behaviors. We don't need to constantly dwell on the past, but we need a clear awareness of those incidents and losses so we can change self-destructive patterns and grow from them.

In *The Grief Factor*, I cover this in greater depth. Research shows that the past matters. A well-documented study on Adverse Childhood Experiences (ACEs) has shown that adults with high ACEs scores frequently have long-term issues with physical and mental health, relationships, and work performance. However, the research on post-traumatic growth shows that past adversity can also be a powerful catalyst for improvement and healing. Having been in the disaster and trauma world for the past 30 years, I've known many people who had horrible childhoods and yet have used those painful experiences for growth. They have become some of the world's most compassionate and effective people helpers.

"Hurt people hurt people," as they say, but hurt people can also heal people! What makes the difference? Those who confront their past can determine that they will use those experiences to achieve amazing growth and transformation. That doesn't mean they won't struggle. They don't just sit by passively and let their past loss or trauma drive their behaviors. Instead, they choose to face their trauma and deal with the loss. In doing so, they define it instead of letting it define them. And along with God and the support of a healthy community of faith throughout this process, amazing things can happen over time.

After one of my classes, a pastor named Joe asked if we could talk. In class I had talked about the Life Impact Timeline, and he told me that his therapist had recommended that he do this exercise. He said it was the most important thing he had done. He had been a pastor for many years, but suddenly found his life falling apart and he couldn't figure out why. He just couldn't cope anymore. He was making some poor decisions that had resulted in his leaving ministry. After doing the exercise, he realized that he had never dealt with the day when, as a teenager, he saw his dad come home, get a piece of water hose, and leave in the car. The police later found him in his car, dead from carbon monoxide fumes pulled in through the hose. Years later, Joe was at a funeral for a relative when his uncle told him that his dad had killed himself primarily because Joe didn't want to carry on the family business.

Joe had never processed his feelings about his dad's death. He had just stuffed them as part of his responsibility of being the oldest child and having to help take care of the family. Avoiding this hard truth had led to numerous issues in his relationships and ministry that he was totally unaware of. Doing the Life Impact exercise helped him identify some negative patterns that had plagued him for years. Consequently, he also discovered that his traumatic loss had made him stronger in ways he had never acknowledged, and that God had brought some amazing people into his life to sustain him and help him grow. The last time I saw him, he was doing well, had a great marriage, and was in a top leadership position in his church denomination.

The Life Impact Timeline

The Life Impact Timeline reflection exercise is a simple assignment, but not an easy one. It isn't something you can do in 15 minutes. You may want to break it up into smaller segments to reflect and process. Like many of the exercises in this workbook, it's something you need to sit with and digest. I call this "soak time." I usually have my clients take two weeks between sessions when they work on this. You might prefer to do it over a weekend or on a vacation where you can be in nature. A mixture of journaling, reflective stillness, and exercise (like walking in nature) can be quite an effective combination. Many people find that being by the water, whether a babbling brook or the waves of an ocean, can be extremely therapeutic.

Completing the Life Impact Timeline exercise can help you:

> Define the people and experiences that shaped you

> Identify common adverse actions you took as a result

> Understand head, heart, and body impacts

> Discover lessons learned

› Identify barriers to growth

› Assess how past events made you stronger

› Reflect on what you still may need to grieve

› Leverage the past to attain higher levels of resilience and post-incident growth

If your past traumas involve some shared experiences with someone else, you might want to get away with the other person for a weekend if possible. You can say, "Hey I'm working through some stuff, and we really never talked about . . ."

Be aware that this exercise can stir up emotions, so you may want to schedule more frequent sessions to process any troubling discoveries you uncover. From a coaching perspective, the focus will be on how your past is impacting you now. You can also mine the tool to identify limiting patterns and behaviors and to chart a course for growth. If you need to process the past more in depth, you may be better served to find a good therapist who is experienced in helping the grieving.

You'll find a copy of the timeline in this workbook, although most people prefer to have more space. You can download copies of the timeline from the resource section of our website (resetlifecoaching.net), then use several copies to extend the timeline over multiple periods of your life.

Start by trying to recall all the major events of your life, both positive and negative, and write them on the appropriate spot on your timeline. Some people like to start at birth and work forward; others start at the present and work backward. After you work through the exercise, I suggest you regularly review the timeline and add new events as they come to mind.

I often challenge people to think about their lives in periods of 20-year segments. Thus, they will use a separate timeline for each 20-year span. I've had some people who had so many critical events that they split some segments into ten years per page of the timeline.

Several people refer to their different life segments as chapters, and some give each one a title. One woman titled a chapter "Chaos;" another man reflected on his early childhood during a period he called "The Sad Little Boy." As you process the important incidents of your past, you should gain a better understanding of their impact on your life. This process can be very enlightening.

Rating Each Event

You will see a vertical scale from 10 to -10 to the left of the timeline. The scale above the timeline is to rate events that impacted you in a positive way. The scale below the line is for things that impacted you in a negative way. I encourage you to first list all the events you can remember and designate a number that first comes to mind for how it impacted you at the time of the incident. Don't spend a lot of time at this point processing each event. You can go back again after you have completed the timeline and *then* reflect on the key questions for each incident. Often, you will write another number beside the incident to indicate your perspective today.

I urge you to review the negative incidents and how they shaped you, even though they may have been very hard at the time. Looking back, however, you may see how they worked out for good and possibly even became positive life-changing events. In other cases, you may find that situations that affected you both positively and negatively, but you'd never before acknowledged the positive impact. In my case, I always felt a lot of loss from my divorce, yet running a divorce support group has since become a rewarding experience for me. Similarly, the pain and stigma from your past can be very difficult, yet many people I have worked with through the years rediscovered themselves and grew immensely from this Life Impact experience.

Be patient. Sometimes it takes years before people are able to see the positives from their previous painful past… and the church isn't always helpful in this regard. Sometimes inexperienced counselors attempt to push survivors' recovery prematurely without allowing them to first go through the travails of lament and grieving what was lost, giving the grievers a sense that the church is not okay when *they* are not okay.

Rebuilding too fast before recognizing the impact of the loss can lead to hasty decisions. This is especially true in relationships. For example, older men often tend to marry too quickly after loss and struggle to establish a fulfilling second marriage like their first one had been.

The reason this exercise is so powerful is that it gives hope and a starting point toward rebuilding. It's a foundational method of rebuilding your life after loss during which a lot of healing can occur.

Sample Life Impact Timeline

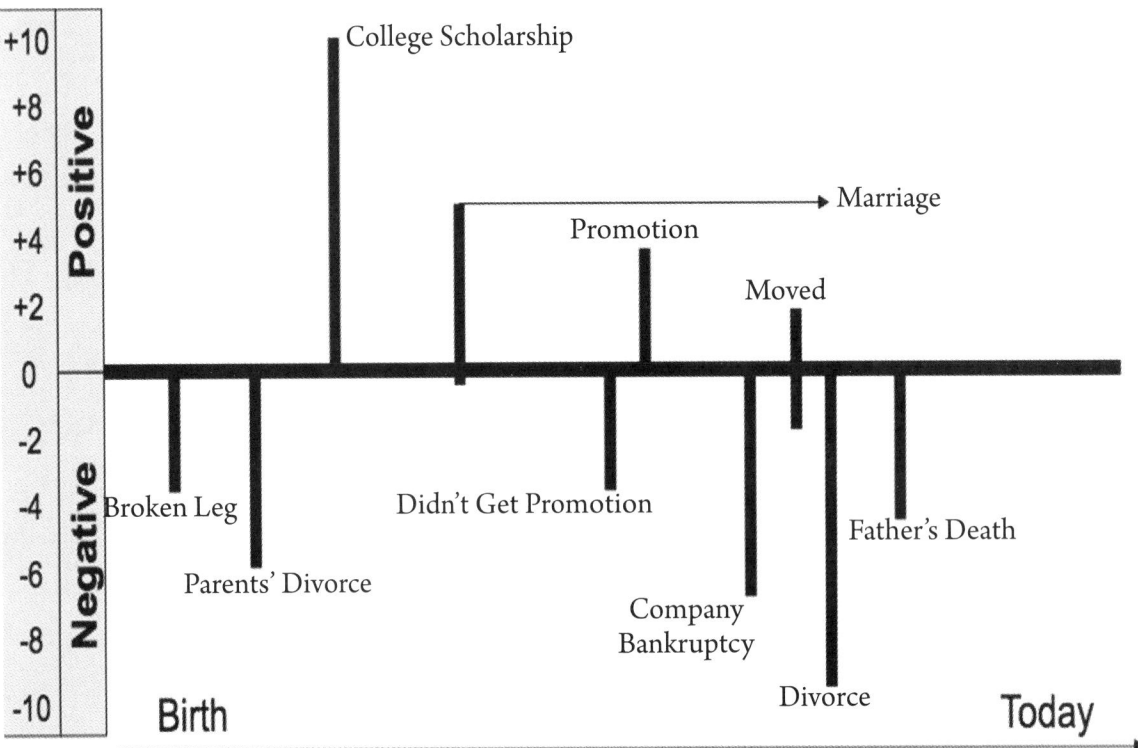

On the next page, you'll find a larger version of the timeline. I put it sideways so you'll have more room to write. Take some time now to jot down the positive and painful events in your life, and indicate the severity by the length of the verticle line on the horizontal line. (See the sample.) As you go through the rest of this chapter, you'll probably remember other events. Come back to the timeline and include them. By the end of this chapter, you'll have a graphic depiction of the times that have brought joy and those that have caused heartache.

Your Life Impact Timeline

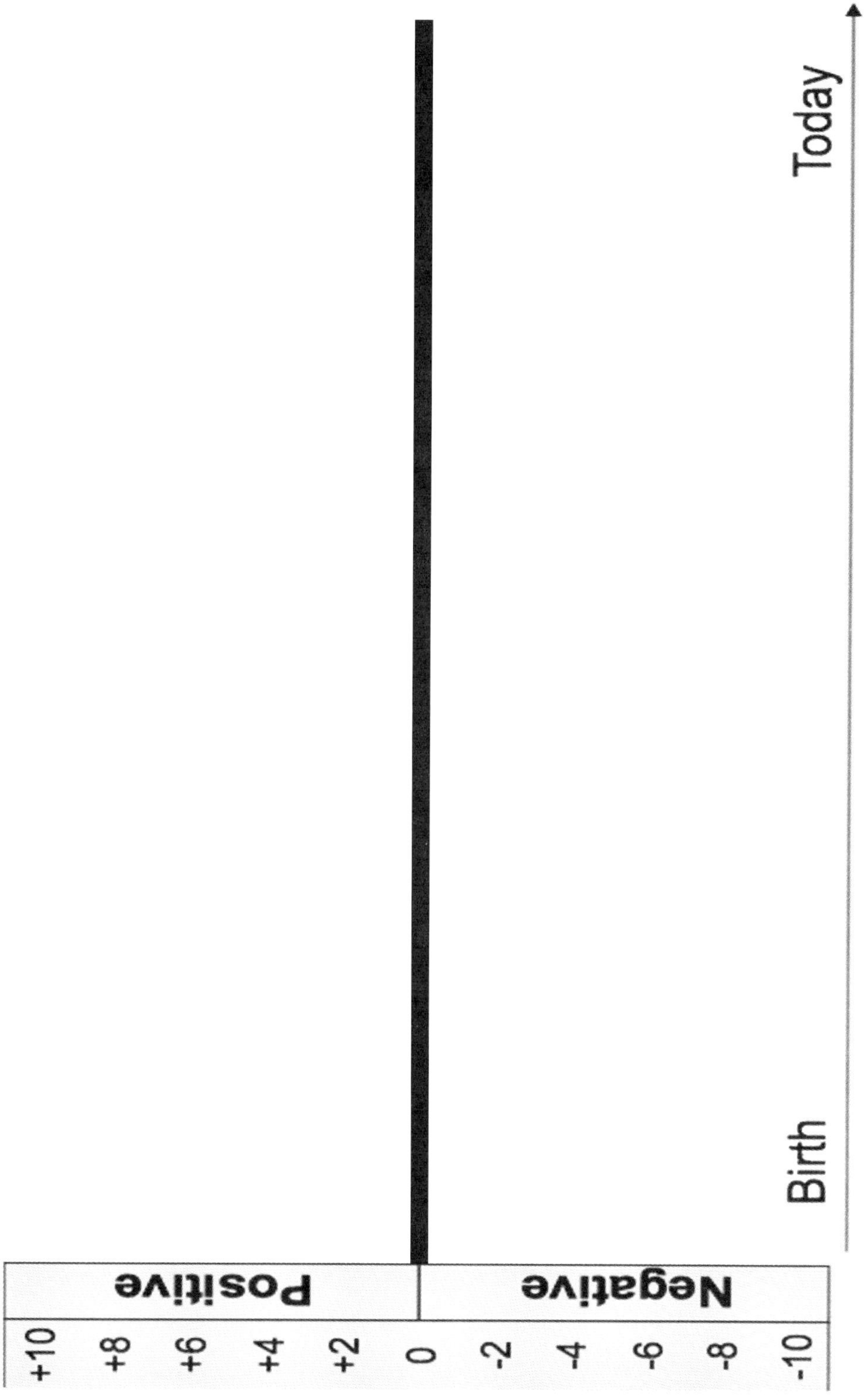

Key Questions

The questions below are very important for you to process as you complete your Life Impact Timeline…if enough time has passed since the incident. If your loss is recent, you aren't likely to have enough perspective to answer some of these yet. You don't need to apply every question to every incident. Review each incident individually and select the questions that are most appropriate. The higher your rating of the event, the more questions will likely apply.

Occasionally you may be surprised when an incident you didn't even consider as significant will provide unexpected insight. One young lady with a history of choosing the wrong men made an important discovery in doing this exercise after a sexual assault. Her "aha moment" was when she realized that she had consistently chosen men who were much like her troubled and estranged brother whom she loved very much as a child. She saw that she was trying to work through her absent relationship with him through these men. She wanted intimacy and friendship, but they wanted more. She realized how this unprocessed and unrecognized loss was subconsciously driving her relationships and causing problems.

Initial Questions

Take some undistracted time to put yourself back in the moment when you experienced the loss.

1. What is the incident and what is its impact?

2. What was the hardest thing about this incident?

3. Did any losses or traumas go unrecognized and/or unacknowledged?

4. How did others around you respond to these incidents? Were you supported?

Questions to Process After Some Time Has Passed

Now, look back on your experience of grief and answer these questions.

1. What did you learn from this event? (Think about self-perception, others, the world, and God)

2. Looking back now, can you identify positives that came from this incident that you didn't see at the time?

3. How did it change you?

4. What did you do with this incident? Where is it currently positioned in your life?

5. On a scale of 1 (not at all) to 10 (very much), how much is it still negatively impacting your life?

6. What would you like to do with what you have learned?

In this workbook, I strongly encourage you to look at the past, present, and future. Acknowledgment of the past is important, but your primary focus should be on the present and future if you want to experience the highest levels of post-loss (post-trauma) growth. You are likely to get more from this exercise if you process with someone else. Having another person validate your experience and observations is critical. It is remarkable how verbally retelling the experience makes it real and allows you to start dealing with it at a different level.

It may seem impossible for a huge loss to result in anything positive during the early stages of grief. We tend to avoid dealing with our grief. However, both grievers and researchers tell us that long-term avoidance of grief isn't healthy. Avoidance of grief doesn't promote growth. Remind yourself that grief can be a powerful catalyst for growth. Dietrich Bonhoeffer explained:

> Nothing can make up for the absence of someone whom we love…it is nonsense to say that God fills the gap; God doesn't fill it, but on the contrary, God keeps it empty and so helps us to keep alive our former communion with each other, even at the cost of pain…The dearer and richer our memories, the more difficult the separation. But gratitude changes the pangs of memory into a tranquil joy. The beauties of the past are borne, not as a thorn in the flesh, but as a precious gift in themselves.[3]

Every loss is different, and the way we experience each loss is different. Remember: a loss is not necessarily a *death*. We will discuss this more later in the book.

Loss Reflection Exercise

After you complete the Life Impact Timeline, take some time to review it. Look at the incidents and make a list of the secondary losses you have experienced due to each primary loss. As an example, if your husband of 20 years died, you may have experienced losses like friendship, companionship, a sexual partner, a co-parent, exercise partner, gardener, protector, and repair man. If you lost your job unexpectedly due to a company being bought out by another, your secondary losses might be normal routine, finances, friends, and lifestyle.

1. What secondary losses were associated with each of the losses you experienced?

2. Which losses were hardest to deal with? Why?

Your Observation About Others' Grief

Many cultures of the world have a healthy grasp of loss and grief, but our culture is grief-averse. We avoid it like the plague! In some ways, that's perfectly understandable because no one seeks the experience of loss. After decades of experiencing my own losses, analyzing the research, and specializing in trauma and grief work surrounding loss in many settings and cultures, my views about grief have changed significantly. The most profound lessons I've learned come from thousands of hours of sitting with the grieving and holding space for them.

In the sacred presence of the grieving, I have developed profound appreciation and understanding of how grief can be a catalyst for growth and transformation. Soon after the initial pain of significant loss, it's very hard to imagine that anything good can come from our grief, but it can—and will. Be patient with yourself and hold on to hope.

1. List other people you have known who experienced grief similar to yours.

2. How did each person experience grief? Did they finally readjust, heal, and have a good life?

3. Who was the best example of rebounding after grief? What was that person's strategy? You may want to take him or her out for coffee and have a chat. Remember, seek the counsel of a variety of people. You don't want to adopt the perspective of a negative Nellie who has spent the last 30 years in a bad state and now complains about it all the time. However, such a person can be a powerful reminder of what you could end up like if you don't do your work!

CHAPTER 3

GRIEF AND PERSONALITY

Therefore, since we have a great high priest who has ascended into heaven, Jesus the Son of God, let us hold firmly to the faith we profess. For we do not have a high priest who is unable to empathize with our weaknesses, but we have one who has been tempted in every way, just as we are—yet he did not sin. Let us then approach God's throne of grace with confidence, so that we may receive mercy and find grace to help us in our time of need.

HEBREWS 4:14-16

Grief Discovery

Healthy grievers are aware that people grieve differently and seek to facilitate the individual needs of each person.

Many years ago I was working with a couple who had experienced the death of their adult son by suicide. The mother's grief was overwhelming and she was crying all the time. In contrast, her husband was a very calm and quiet man who seemed to have experienced little change in his functioning. During one session she looked at him and said, "I just don't understand you! I'm falling apart. I can barely function, and you just seem to go on without being impacted at all. I know you loved our son as much as I did, but I don't get it."

I asked the man to talk about his grief experience and how he was processing it. He said he had been spending a lot of time in his basement workshop because he and his son had spent hours there building furniture together. He was making pieces of furniture and other items as mementos of their son to give to friends and family members so they would remember him. He explained how he felt close to their son when he was there, but hadn't realized his withdrawal was making his wife feel alone, and even abandoned. As they talked, it became clear that his grief was primarily an intellectual response while hers was emotional. This was consistent with their personalities.

We discussed what each was experiencing and what they needed from each other. She needed to emote a lot, but the intensity of her emotions was difficult for him to handle. He was able to explain that he needed to process things cognitively. It wasn't that he didn't want to be there for her. It was just that he grieved very differently. He didn't know how to make her feel better, and her grief made him feel helpless. Meanwhile, she didn't have the mental capacity to process his grief with him. As she put it, "My brain just isn't working right."

After this conversation and an exploration of options, we were able to get her in a grief support group. She found a good counselor to help her experience and process her grief in a meaningful and healing way. He didn't need the group support. He preferred solitude as he physically worked through his grief and processed it in his head. The differences in their grief experience were dividing them instead of uniting them, but they were finally able to find some times and ways to experience their grief together that worked for them.

Patterns of Experiencing and Expressing Grief

People are often confused about why their experience with grief doesn't fit the pattern of others they know. It helps to realize that people can process the same sorrowful experience in very different ways. In this chapter we will look at three ways: in the head, in the heart, or in the body. We all utilize all three dimensions, but one is likely to be the primary way. Some of us are more blended grievers than others.

One of the big problems I have discovered in working with grievers is that when we're hurting, we expect others to know what we need and how to meet those needs. However, we rarely are specific about what these needs are. Consequently, we get hurt and frustrated, and may even feel abandoned when our needs aren't met. I frequently observe this in married couples, as in the opening example.

When you feel like others aren't there for you in the way you would desire, start by asking yourself these two questions:

1. When people ask me how they can help, do I make it clear *how* they can best help?

2. Do *I* even know what I need?

We can encounter a surprising number of obstacles in trying to determine what we need and what others can do to help us while we're grieving. This might be a first-time experience you're forced to deal with, so you don't know what might help. Perhaps you have learned unhealthy patterns from growing up in a dysfunctional family. Maybe you're usually the designated caregiver in the family and no one else is informed or prepared when *you* need help.

If so, keep calm. Try not to panic. Grief has a way of guiding you inward. You are "fearfully and wonderfully made" by a loving God. If you stop and listen for his voice, you will usually know what you need to do.

Healthy grievers take responsibility for their own grief and don't have unrealistic expectations of others. Don't sit passively soaking in anger and rejection, waiting for others to help you feel better. That is a surefire recipe for getting stuck and can easily lead to resentment. Remind yourself that this is your loss and your grief journey. Others might be companions on segments of that journey, but it is yours to traverse.

People experience grief very differently. In their books, Terry Martin and Kenneth Doka describe a continuum of grief, with instrumental (physical/cognitive) grief at one end and intuitive (emotional) grief at the other.[4] A grieving person might be at either end of the continuum, or at any point between, blending both aspects. I thought their terminology might be confusing for some, so I differentiate between "head grievers" (cognitive) and "heart grievers" (emotional). Look at the two following lists and put a checkmark beside the descriptions that you feel relate to your grief style.

Head Grievers	Heart Grievers
☐ Focus on cognition/moderated affect; shared common feelings with intuitive grievers, though feelings are less intense	☐ Focus on affect over cognition
☐ Brief periods of cognitive dysfunction are common	☐ Longer term cognitive impairment as there may be prolonged periods of confusion, inability to concentrate, disorganization, and disorientation
☐ A desire to master environment; thus a majority of grief energy is focused on problem-solving and planned activities as an adaptive strategy	☐ Less likely than head grievers to seek out potential problems and solve them
☐ A general reluctance to discuss feelings	☐ Feelings are intensely experienced Expressions such as crying and lamenting mirror inner experience
☐ Grief is more an intellectual experience	
☐ May initially respond by explaining the circumstance of their losses rather than to how they are feeling	☐ Grief expressed is a grief experienced
	☐ Go with the experience of grief
☐ May experience grief physically as augmented energy which takes the form of restlessness or nervousness	☐ Majority of grief energy is focused on feelings—less energy for cognition
	☐ Successful adaptive strategies facilitate the experience and expression of feeling
☐ May be unaware of internal arousal	☐ Physical exhaustion and/or anxiety may result
☐ May feel disenfranchised as others do not accept their grief pattern	☐ May feel that others do not allow for adequate expression of their grief
☐ May be uncomfortable with the strong expressed emotions of others	☐ May be unable or unwilling to distance oneself from feelings expressed by others

What does this exercise tell you about your grief style?

Grief Style Reflection Exercise

Often you will find yourself around others whom you feel are not being helpful or are at a loss as to how to help you. It may be because they are at the opposite end of the grief continuum. Helpful self-reflection on the following questions can lead to conversations with others who care and want to help you get the support you need.

What are the primary signs that I am not doing okay and need support?

1.

2.

3.

4.

When I am experiencing grief, what I need most is . . .

1.

2.

3.

4.

I was recently working with a grieving family. The oldest sibling confided that he just didn't understand the way his sisters were grieving the death of their father. They had all watched his health decline gradually over several years. Early in the process, the son had come to terms that his father was going to die. He had made an effort to spend time with his father and he felt he was doing well in the aftermath of his death. Several of his sisters, however, had not accepted that their father might die. They had held out hope for recovery until the day of his death. It was obvious that their grief was just starting, but the son's had started two years prior. Therapists call this *anticipatory grief*. The son still grieved after his father died, of course, yet he had done most of his grief work prior to the death. As a primarily head type of griever, he struggled to connect with his sisters. He found it challenging and disturbing to be around their raw, high emotions. He also felt that they were judging him as being insensitive and uncaring.

Helping families understand both the head and heart perspectives on grief is something they find most helpful. Making this distinction early in the grieving process can help prevent a lot of pain and resentment. If your family has a history of difficulty and dysfunction, you probably need someone to sit down and facilitate this with you all. But if your family is somewhat healthy emotionally, you may be able to do it yourself. You might begin by saying, "We all have different personalities and see life from different perspectives. Therefore, we may grieve differently. I want to be there for you and don't want to assume that you want or need the same things I do. Let me tell you how this has impacted me, how I am struggling, and what I think I need most. Then you can do the same."

But be forewarned; not all families can do this! If your family can't seem to come together and provide the support that everyone needs, you may have friends or coworkers who can be there for you. When they ask how they can help you, let them know!

The next chapter will continue to explore support systems. But first, take some time to reflect on these questions:

1. What type of griever am I?

2. What type of grievers are in my world? Do I grieve differently from them? Have others accepted my style of grief?

3. What do others who've experienced this same loss need from me?

4. How can I best experience and mourn this loss in a way that is helpful?

CHAPTER 4

SUPPORT SYSTEMS DURING GRIEF

Praise be to the God and Father of our Lord Jesus Christ, the Father of compassion and the God of all comfort, who comforts us in all our troubles, so that we can comfort those in any trouble with the comfort we ourselves receive from God. For just as we share abundantly in the sufferings of Christ, so also our comfort abounds through Christ.

2 CORINTHIANS 1:3-5

Grief Discovery

Healthy grievers carefully assess their support system and seek to surround themselves by people who can help facilitate their grief, growth, and emotional and spiritual wellness.

I will always remember a woman I met at the Salvation Army disaster relief effort after the 9/11 terrorist attack at the World Trade Center. A huge operation had been established to provide food, hydration, snacks, and emotional and spiritual care to the first responders and workers involved in the cleanup and recovery efforts. This woman stood out as she walked around cleaning the tables, checking on people, and spreading kindness and love. After a few days of seeing her humble service, I took a break with her and commended her on the good work she was doing. During our conversation I discovered that her son had died in one of the towers. She said she had stepped forward to do what she could do "instead of just sitting around in her house grieving." She went on to tell me that helping others was really helping her through her grief. She felt like she was making a small difference in the face of overwhelming tragedy. Her pain had motivated her to serve with higher levels of compassion—and it was evident.

Not everyone can recover so quickly in the immediate aftermath of such a devastating loss. In fact, one of one of the pre-deployment questions we ask potential crisis responders is if they've had a recent loss or traumatic event in their life. We don't want them to be crying louder than the person they are trying to help! However, the woman in this situation was doing an amazing job while actively serving in her grief.

Surrounded by Helpers, but Feeling Alone

Before I started working with people in grief, I naively believed that when a great tragedy hit, sufferers' friends and family would surround them with loving support. I assumed that appropriate people in their lives would show up for them, understand what they needed, and provide appropriate care as long as necessary. Boy, was I wrong! I quickly discovered that some grievers felt alone even when surrounded by many well-meaning family, friends, and other connections. Some were deeply hurt by the actions (or inactions) of "helpers" who seemed not to understand their grief. Others felt shunned, rejected, judged, and invalidated in their pain. Ironically, sometimes their spiritual leaders seemed ill-equipped to help, which was surprising to me. It was very common for grievers to feel they were being pushed too quickly to recover from their grief and "get back to normal."

One of the things you may be saddened to discover when you're grieving is that many people have a limited capacity to accompany you on your grief journey. This can be incredibly painful when you're feeling so vulnerable. When you are hurt by the actions or inactions of others after a loss, we call it "secondary wounding"—it's much like being hit by "friendly fire" in a military battle.

Try to understand that while a few people really don't care and have no desire to support you, others simply aren't able to help because they don't have the emotional or relational capacity. This is the time for you to take inventory of your prospects. Do you have realistic expectations for how others will support you? Life is busy and your friends and family have competing demands on their time. Some will have many more emotional needs than others, so you may need to spread yourself out a little bit if you are seeing signs of them pulling away and setting boundaries.

Remember that you are responsible for yourself and your own healing. Think of yourself as a sponge. Do you constantly try to suck up the energy of others around you? That's not a healthy strategy. A sponge is made to absorb water, but you're expected to stop occasionally to wring it out well. Even in your grief, you need to pour life into others.

I don't want you to lose hope because many grievers are also surprised by the new relationships that transpire after loss. An interesting fact is that as we pour ourselves into others, our efforts have a way of benefiting us as well. Scripture says, "Give, and it will be given to you. A good measure, pressed down, shaken together and running over, will be poured into your lap. For with the measure you use, it will be measured to you" (Luke 6:38). This verse is often applied to finances, but that is not the focus of the passage. It is found in a context of not judging, loving one's enemies, and showing forgiveness (Luke 6:32-37). Basically, the principle is that if you go beyond your own concerns and give to others, you too will be rewarded. Healthy grievers are able to both give and receive.

Your experience of grief may be nothing like anyone else's that you know. People vary in their capacity to function in the immediate aftermath of a tragedy. But regardless of how you respond initially, as time goes on, reconnection with others is important.

Solitude vs. Loneliness

People also vary broadly in the amount of social interaction they desire and need. It is very common to turn inward and withdraw socially after loss or while in a state of deep grief. Even when physically present with others, it may feel as if you are not socially, emotionally, or relationally connected.

Have you ever stood in a room packed with people and felt totally alone and unnoticed? Have you ever wished everyone else would just go away so you could sit in silence with your dog for a while? Can you tell when people are trying (and failing) to help you through a painful experience by doing what they would like someone to do for them in the same circumstances? You can't blame them for trying, but they just don't understand that everyone's grief is different, and not all pain will be resolved with the same approach.

It's important to make a distinction between social isolation, solitude, and loneliness. Let's consider these key terms.

Loneliness is a distressing feeling that results when your desire or need to interact with certain individuals or people in general goes unfulfilled. Dr. Vivek H. Murthy, 19th and 21st Surgeon General of the United States, recently released an interesting finding on loneliness. Research shows that half the adults in America reported experiencing loneliness—and that was before the impacts of the COVID-19 pandemic that further isolated many of us from friends, loved ones, and support systems, increasing isolation and exacerbating loneliness. Murthy states, "Loneliness is far more than just a bad feeling—it harms both individual and societal health. It is associated with a greater risk of cardiovascular disease, dementia, stroke, depression, anxiety, and premature death."

The mortality impact of being socially disconnected is similar to that caused by smoking up to 15 cigarettes a day, and even greater than that associated with obesity and physical inactivity. The harmful consequences of a society that lacks social connection can be felt in our schools, workplaces, and civic organizations, where performance, productivity, and engagement are diminished.

Murthy notes: "But loneliness is a subjective term about how you feel about your connection. I might have one person around me but not feel lonely at all because I feel a deep connection to myself and that person. Or I could have one hundred people around me and feel profoundly lonely which happens to many people. We could ensure that people are interacting with others all day long, but that doesn't mean we will reduce loneliness."[5]

Solitude may be defined simply as a state of being alone. Loneliness is subjective; not everyone who is alone feels lonely. Solitude is objective; everyone who is alone experiences solitude. Loneliness is an unpleasant feeling, but many people go out of their way to create periods of solitude where they can get away from the noise of the surrounding world and hear themselves think.

As I write this chapter, I have just returned from three weeks of nonstop travel and interacting with people. Much of that time, I was in front of crowds who wanted to hear what I was saying. I'm an extrovert and love being around people, but the older I get, the more I crave the solitude and stillness of my little farm. Nothing is more life-giving for me than when I sit where I am right now, barefoot in the glider in my backyard, writing. It is summer, and in a few hours I will write while watching the sun fall into the trees while my horses, goats, cats, donkey, and chickens come around me to graze and just hang out.

Social isolation may be defined as having few social relationships, social roles, group memberships, and infrequent social interaction.[6]

I recall an event where I was sitting with some colleagues when a woman on the other side of the table saw someone walk in and immediately traded seats with another person at our table so she wouldn't have to sit by that person. It reminded me of my childhood. I grew up in a part of the country where certain groups practiced *shunning*—a community-wide attempt to ban certain individuals from participating in public gatherings. The shunned person is deliberately avoided by groups and individuals. Shunning shows public disapproval of another's actions or some other factor like race, culture, socioeconomic status, gender, etc. (Being shunned can be highly distressing to not only humans, but also animals. I've seen horses run out of the herd for bad behavior.)

Growing up in that community had an effect on me. I recently attended an event where I didn't know anyone. As I walked into the room for a mixer, most everyone was already paired up or in small groups engaged in conversation. I mentally flashed back to how insecure and lonely I would have felt years ago. Now, however, I didn't feel that way. (I hope I'm getting wiser as I get older.) Instead, since I didn't see anyone else who appeared to be as awkwardly alone as I was, I got some food, walked over to the window, and looked out at the beauty of spring. While immersed in scanning the landscape, someone else walked up to look out the window and we made a natural and enjoyable connection.

People who have recently lost a spouse or have gone through a painful divorce often find it difficult to walk alone into a restaurant, church, or social setting. They aren't being shunned, but it can feel like it. They feel like outsiders, like they don't belong with all the enthusiastic friends and groups inside. At best, they likely feel like a "third wheel" now as a single person instead of a couple. Their social isolation is self-imposed, but still emotionally painful.

Other social isolation can be intentional, or at least appear that way. I've heard many stories from grievers about how others intentionally avoided them. Someone might be at a grocery store and see someone they know start to turn down their aisle, but then do an abrupt about-face and go down another aisle instead. In working with grievers, I point out that most people aren't intentionally hurtful in their actions, yet many are careless and insensitive. Often, when people just don't know what to say to a grieving person, they (mistakenly) think their next best option is to avoid him or her.

It is important, however, to remember that when your grief is fresh, you may be extra-sensitive and prone to misinterpret things. This may push some people away because they are afraid of saying or doing something to accidentally increase your suffering. Or the person in the grocery may truly not have seen you and perhaps turned around because he had forgotten something. You can expend a lot of energy and postpone the healing process by trying to get support from someone who can't or won't provide it.

Finding the Right People with the Right Advice

Grief has a way of helping you reevaluate your relationships. Don't be surprised if your circle of friends changes and you develop a stronger support system in the aftermath. It is a great time to purge your life of toxic and unhealthy relationships. You may also strengthen other friendships that you have taken for granted. You will likely form new relationships with greater depth and maturity. Your worldview, priorities, and interests will change, so you may no longer relate to everyone the way you did previously. Some people will seem shallow; others will exhibit a depth and quality that you hadn't previously recognized or appreciated.

In my research with grievers and those trying to support them, these are some of the most common reasons people find it difficult to provide appropriate support.

> They have never experienced a huge loss, so they can't relate to the pain.

> Your grief reminds them of their own unresolved losses that they have never grieved.

> Your method of grieving is very different from theirs and they don't know how to relate to you or help you.

> Perhaps you make it hard for them to know how to help you.

> The people in your life and the family dynamic make it difficult to adjust to your loss and behavioral change.

> They don't know what to say.

It is critical to have reliable and consistent support from others during your grief journey. Now that you know whom you need to sidestep for now, what kind of people *should* you be looking for? A great grief companion will:

> Be present with you whatever state you are in.

> Keep your story confidential.

> Balance doing things *for* you with doing things *with* you.

> Meet you where you are, but love you too much to let you self-destruct.

> Love you at all times, but speak truth when needed.

> Refrain from judging you when you don't "get it right."

> Be with you without trying to "fix you."

> Be patient and not push you to "get over it" or "get back to normal."

> Challenge you when you need it.

> Listen.

> Be vulnerable and share their own struggles without hijacking your story and making it all about them.

After reviewing the list above, it can be beneficial to review your Life Impact Timeline and mine it to discover people who will be helpful during your grief journey. Look at the crisis situations you've experienced in the past and see who provided positive support. When I am on scene with someone immediately after a loss, it is one of the first things that I do. I can help them with this within minutes after the tragedy strikes.

When faced with a devastating event, everyone needs to be connected with others who are helpful. So spend a few minutes now and consider:

1. As I've faced various difficulties in the past, who was there for me? (Make a list.)

2. Who else do I know who exhibits most of the qualities of a great grief companion?

3. When and how can I connect with the people who can offer me the best support in the current stage of my grief journey?

STRATEGIC GRIEVING: MOURNING RITUALS, CEREMONIES, AND ACTIVITIES

"Blessed are those who mourn, for they will be comforted."

MATTHEW 5:4

Grief Discovery

Healthy grievers strategically engage in activities that help facilitate grieving for healing and growth.

As an emergency response chaplain, I frequently encounter people who seem to be absolutely clueless about what to do after someone dies. In my earlier years, that was seldom a problem. Most people were tied to some faith-based group, and even if those ties were loose ones, the church was there to offer support and structure to its grieving members. In addition, the community had traditions that guided friends and relatives through the death of a loved one. Grievers could attend viewings or wakes, and hold a funeral where everyone was able to mourn together while saying goodbye to the recently departed. People were more connected then.

In the past decade, I have seen this change. Fewer are involved in any community of faith, and many have little cultural affiliation. It is concerning to observe societal changes for grievers in recent years. A major shift has been made from the traditional funeral to more of a celebration of life, which is often a much less somber occasion. I suspect that the "supporters" of the bereaved often try too hard to keep the focus of the celebration only on positive memories of the deceased. They attempt to keep things lighthearted, hoping to minimize emotional pain. But somewhere in the process, grief demands solemnity. I fear that when celebrations of life effectively ignore any mention of death, they only postpone the surviving person's need to grieve deeply.

Mourning rituals don't have rules, of course, yet they are important to us as humans. They facilitate our need to address the great mystery of death in observable and participatory ways, and they enable us to ask questions and express genuine feelings of sorrow, doubt, and fear. Rituals surrounding death offer important elements of comfort to grievers by bringing people together. When you lose someone or something of great meaning to you, it is important to acknowledge that loss. If you're staring down at a motionless body in a casket, surrounded by others who have come to view it with you, you begin to actively engage with your grief and start facing the reality of the loss. It's a first big step toward growth and healing.

In this chapter I will outline some exercises that I do with my clients, or they've done on their own, that they found helpful. You don't need to do all of them—and not any of them until you are ready. However, I'm providing them here as options to get your creative juices flowing.

See What Works...See What Doesn't

Take ample time to reflect on what you feel you need to do to mourn your loss. The things that others around you do may or may not be helpful to you. What is helpful to one person may not be helpful for another, even among family members. After the loss of a son, the dad may want to spend time at the gravesite. However, the mom may not feel any connection with her son at his grave.

Think about the cultural setting surrounding your grief. If grievers don't have any helpful cultural rituals to help them through their period of grief, it's perfectly okay if they want to borrow a ritual from another culture or create a new idea that feels right for their loss and their grief.

Don't attempt to rush your grieving process. It will last longer for some people than for others. Sometimes it may feel like the world puts a time frame on your grief. In our western culture, we prefer a microwave to a slow cooker, but grief is not a microwave experience. (This is one of the biggest frustrations I hear from grievers.)

Society also has a limited tolerance for grief and mourning. Just in case you are wondering, three days of bereavement leave is not enough! An all-too-common experience is for someone to return to work too soon and face the inevitable encounters in the break room with coworkers asking, "Hey, how are you doing?" If you dare to actually attempt a real conversation and tell them the truth—that right now your life totally sucks and you would rather join your loved one in death than have to come back to this crummy job—you'll get that look. You know the one, the "Oh crap, what do I say now?" look. Soon you learn to say "I'm okay." It's a lie. You know it (and so do they), but where can you really tell the truth?

The church has a wonderful opportunity to minister to people in times of grief. The elements of faith combined with compassion invite grievers to not only face the reality of the finality of this life, but to then look ahead with hope to the life to come. A young widow decided to dive into her grief after her husband died of cancer, and she chose to be vulnerable about what she was feeling. At the next church service when others asked how she was doing, she told them she wasn't doing well and, actually, didn't want to live anymore without her husband. She trusted an amazing group of people who were able to listen, be present, and create space for her grief. I wish everyone had that type of community where real conversations could take place.

The church can provide a turning point between today's harsh reality and a promised new reality as we seek to rebuild a new life. For the Christian, death is not final; it is just an end to our physical presence on this earth. Within a Christian community, grievers can find not only support, but lasting comfort, hope, and strength for their journey ahead.

If you aren't involved in such a community, you may have to create one of your own. It doesn't have to be some formally endorsed program at a church. Look at your list of friends and ask two of them if they will join you in supporting each other. Come up with some guidelines. Maybe start with these:

We will:

- Treat each other with unconditional love.
- Speak truth only in the context of love.
- Seek to be dispensers of grace rather than judgment.
- Embrace our own imperfection.
- Be patient with each other and not make comparisons to another's journey.
- Hold each other up in prayer.

› Hold each other accountable in specific ways requested by each person.

› Sacredly hold what is revealed in confidence—not sharing with anyone, including spouses.

› Challenge each other toward emotional, spiritual, and relational wellness with God, family, and others.

Whether you want it to or not, life goes on after loss. At some point you have to go back to work or your old routine. If you have kids, they need parenting. Bills have to be paid. The lawn has to be mowed. Groceries have to be purchased. You may not do these mundane things as willingly as you did before. Indeed, you may prefer to just pull the covers over your head and pray for a meteor to take out your house. You know you need to put on your big-person-pants and step out into the world, but what happens when you have to perform something hard and your brain just isn't functioning the way it used to?

Healthy grievers try to find a balance. They acknowledge their emotions as they arise and attempt to name and facilitate them as they happen. It's fine and necessary to put your grief on hold for a bit, but that's not always possible. You may be in the grocery store and see a bag of peanuts when *boom*! Grief ambushes you. You suddenly remember sitting with your grandpa in his old farm truck, eating peanuts and "waitin' for the women like always!" Grandpa's gone now, and so are those days that created so many special moments of childhood. Or maybe you're heading into the board meeting when a man walks by wearing the same cologne your recently deceased husband used to wear. You are a puddle and have to hurry into the bathroom stall for a few minutes. It's okay. Let it out. Take deep breaths. Pull it together. It will get better.

The question is, when do you grieve? Healthy grievers allow a space and time for grieving. Those early days after the loss are hard, but you can't stuff it forever and be healthy. In the words of my friend and mentor H. Norman Wright, you will likely "be ambushed when you least expect it."

In looking at the research, one thing is very clear. The consensus among researchers, practitioners, and the bereaved themselves is that there is no single correct or universal way in which each person should experience grief or mourn a loss. It's up to you to create your own plan.

So think about what you need. Do you need an hour every day to walk in the woods and collect your thoughts? That may be hard if you're a single mom. Many single parents with kids discover that carving out "alone time" is difficult, and they find themselves grieving in ten-minute intervals while in the shower with the water streaming down over their tears. You need enough time where you can untangle and experience all your jumbled emotions and then descend into your grief. If you can do this, it will help with facilitating a change in the frequency, intensity, and duration of your grief.

Grieving is healthy and healing, so don't act as if it's something bad. If you have children, you can model for them how to grieve. Remember that they learn how to grieve from watching those around them.

Better Late Than Never

You may have picked up this book because someone close to you died, but in the process of doing some of these exercises you've uncovered other losses that you never grieved. No one may have recognized the loss, not even you. Did anyone show up to help you process your grief when your fur baby (and closest friend of 20 years) died? What about when you were fired from the job you loved, but no one knew how to talk with you about it? It's never too late for a funeral or loss ceremony once you recognize something or someone has died. Some losses go unrecognized for years, but when they finally show up, they demand attention.

If you come to terms with a loss that you never fully addressed, it helps to think of a specific action that acknowledges its "death." I often process this with people and encourage them to think about what would best help them to move on. This practice started in my divorce groups. When I found that a marriage had died and one person had moved on, but the other was still emotionally connected, I would suggest a post-divorce funeral for the wedding that didn't work out. When I'm out on the farm with my RESET Life Coaching practice, I encourage participants to bring a photo of the person (or something else to represent the loss) and we burn it, bury it, or otherwise signify a permanent ending. Sometimes they need to write an obituary or letter. This exercise can be the start of a transition from grieving a loss to rebuilding a life. Children often do well with play therapy, or they may do something with you to facilitate therapeutic play that is far more powerful than talk therapy.

For example, one of my play therapist colleagues was working with a preschool boy whose grandfather had died. The two were very close, but his parents didn't let him go to the funeral. Soon after the death he started having behavioral problems, which was unusual for him. During a play therapy session one day he walked over to the sand table, picked up a male figure, laid him in the sand, covered him over, and said, "Well now, that's done." After briefly processing this with his therapist, he left. Almost immediately afterward, his parents reported the boy had returned to normal behavior and had stopped his acting out. This is a great illustration even for us adults. Sometimes I work with people who have been carrying vestiges of something dead for many years that is causing exhaustion and a stink in their life and relationships. Sometimes you come to the realization that you still need to bury something or someone.

Another way to avoid waiting too long to grieve is to consider preemptive grief. This was my father's idea. When he was dying of cancer I started having conversations with him about what he wanted at his funeral. He had been a pastor all his life and I wanted to honor his wishes. One day he told me, "You know, it's really stupid to have a funeral after you die. You should have your funeral *before* you die." I checked to make sure he was cognizant and then explored this with him more. He went on to explain that after you're dead, all the people you know and love show up, but he wanted to celebrate with them before he died. The more I thought about it, the more it seemed like a good idea.

We decided to have his funeral before he died and called it a celebration of life. (In his case, it truly was!) He had grown up on a farm and was a big John Deere tractor fan, so we decorated with that theme. We made a list of all the people he wanted there and sent invitations to his closest high school, college, and ministry friends, along with family and people in his church. We wheeled his bed from the parsonage across the parking lot to the church where he gave his final words to his wife, children, siblings, friends, parishioners, and even the hospice workers. After the ceremony, one of the pastors in town brought his church band and they played music while we fired up the grill and fellowshipped. It was a time of both sadness and joy. We cried and laughed together in this beautiful and memorable ceremony. We had a small funeral after Dad died, but much of our grieving was already done. Who says you can't have your funeral before you die?

Time for Some Exercises

Continue to give all this information some thought as you begin to put it into practice. Work through the following exercises and see what is most helpful in helping you move forward in your grief.

A Timeline Exercise

In Chapter Two you did a Life Impact Timeline exercise where you outlined significant losses. Go back now and review that timeline in light of what you have learned in the past few chapters. Consider the following:

> Can you recall other losses that weren't previously recognized and identified? If so, add them to the timeline.

> Do you need to revisit any of those losses, talk to someone about them, or perhaps even do a releasing ceremony or ritual? If so, consider these ideas:

- Gather with a few friends to bury or burn something. (Just don't start a wildfire! Make sure you contain it in a firepit, empty metal trash can, or fireplace.)

- Write a letter and maybe read it to someone, even if it is a pet. People like to do that with the horses at my ranch because they are great at holding space, they don't talk, and they keep confidentiality!

- Return to a specific location (alone or with someone else) where something significant occurred in your past.

- Build something in memory of what or who was lost.

- Sponsor a homeless shelter room, create a grant for an underprivileged college student, or support a child in a developing country.

Do any of these ideas "ring true" as something you want to do? If so, carve out some time to get started. If not, what activity will be more meaningful to you?

A Visual Exercise

Below is another grieving exercise that people often find helpful. The purpose of this one is to help you think about your grief journey and the different experiences you've had by laying everything out visually. This exercise can be very healing and facilitate positive internal shifts and forward movement in your grief. It is better if you can process it with someone who can hold sacred space for you. Feel free to draw symbols or figures, search your photos, or find images from old magazines to glue on paper. With modern technology, you may do this on a computer or tablet with some pretty cool apps. You could even use crayons, pencils, or paint if that's your preferred medium.

My Journey of Grief - Oh the places I have been!

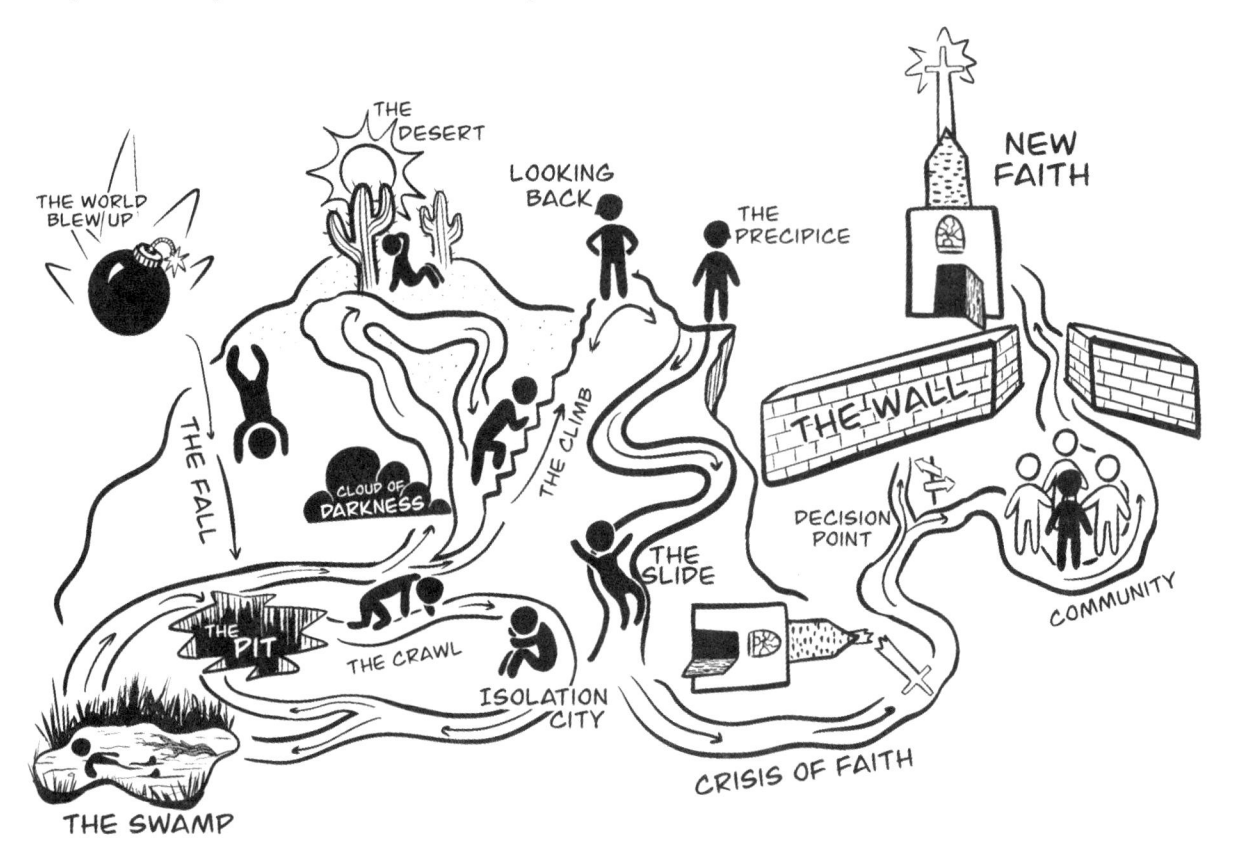

From *The Grief Factor:* Illustrated by Madison Ellers (@madisonoliviaart)

Step One

Most people start at the point of loss in the lower left corner of the paper and progress toward the other side. However, some prefer to start with a picture of what life was like before loss. You may want to start where you are right now and recreate it backward to the point of the loss. Many like to put pictures or names of people who were with them at different legs of the journey or places they passed through. There are no rules with this. This is for you and about you. Life is rarely a straight line, so think about ups and downs, times you circled back or got in a detour or traffic jam. You can use multiple pages or even get a poster board for this exercise. When finished, make sure to take a picture of it. However, don't presume your journey is complete. I hope this will become an ongoing art project as the years go on. I encourage you to reflect, revise it, and add additional pages of the journey as needed! Sometimes people start trying to document their grief journey as soon as they're aware of it. More often, though, I see people using this exercise when they feel they need help or are stuck.

The following list includes some of the common words that people use to describe periods in their grief journey. This is not an exhaustive list; use your own words and descriptions, and put them in the order that reflects your experience.

- Desert—the dry and thirsty land
- Joy Town
- The wilderness
- Precipice
- Raging River runaway boat
- Tidal wave
- The pit
- Lazy River
- The swamp
- Quicksand
- Cloud of darkness
- Isolation point
- Rejection Village
- The storm
- Siberia

- The bridge
- Roadblock
- Decision point—the Y
- The harbor
- Fellow travel companions
- Oasis
- The wall

Step Two

Months or even years from now it can be very helpful to spend time reflecting on these different periods of your grief journey. I encourage you to do this at some point, and I find it is most beneficial to process with someone else. You may want to do this as you hit each segment of the journey, but I usually recommend completing it first and then going back with a bird's-eye view. You don't have to do this for every segment or answer every question, but you are looking for key things that shaped you, such as:

1. What lessons did I learn during this time?

2. What changed about how I viewed the world, God, others, and myself?

3. What were the hardest places for me?

4. What most shaped my growth?

5. What places do I tend to helicopter back to most often?

A Breathing Exercise

We all know the importance of physical breathing, but few of us fully understand how breathing impacts us emotionally. We all breathe to stay alive, but research is showing that few of us breathe well. Most of us are breathing too fast and shallow. The optimum breathing rate is 5.5 breaths per minute. If you find your breathing rate has increased due to a state of stress, you can get it back under control within a few minutes by simply breathing differently. It's pretty easy, but it takes practice.

Try it the next time you're feeling stressed out due to grief or any other reason. To calm yourself down, start by inhaling very slowly through your nose and then exhaling even slower through your mouth. Do three to four rounds of this slow breathing, which should come to about 5.5 breaths per minute. Many YouTube videos demonstrate how to do this if you need further instruction. The benefits of bringing down your breathing rate include lowered blood pressure, increased heart rate variability, and more energy.

On the other hand, if you want to ramp up your nervous system to acquire energy for movement and clarity, take in some deep fast breaths. If you have observed horses, you will see that they do this. When something scares them, their heads go up high and they take in a deep, fast breath.

Depending on your desired result, use the first of these breathing methods to calm your emotional state when it is highly activated, and the second to increase your concentration and energy when you need to attend to a task. I frequently have my clients breathe slowly when they arrive to move into a calmer state. At the end of the session when they are ready to leave, I have them take some deep, fast breaths before they go.

A Meditation Exercise

Another worthwhile way to facilitate your grief is through meditation. When I teach people how to meditate, they often say the experience results in their feeling a significant internal shift. Some people have concerns about meditation and ask if it is biblical. The answer is yes, if it is done right. Christian meditation is not at all like eastern meditation. Although both are designed to help calm the mind and body physiologically, they have some very distinct differences. Eastern meditation promotes emptying the mind and focusing on a mantra—a special word or phrase. Christian meditation, on the other hand, is a form of worship intended to help you enhance your relationship with God. Rather than emptying your mind, you fill it with a deep abiding awareness of the presence of God which can help you reduce stress, relieve anxiety, and process grief. Unfortunately, Christian meditation was not a discipline I practiced in my early adult life. Only after experiencing my own losses and working with other grievers did I discover the power of meditation in grief healing.

Each person is unique and God may lead you to adapt this practice as you move through your grief. If so, find a quiet place without the distraction of other humans if possible. Animals are fine. I first learned about the power of meditation by spending time with horses and being part of the herd. I later found I could experience a profound shift by sitting with the horses or elsewhere out in God's creation—especially beside ocean waves or near running water.

Weather permitting, go outside and sit with your feet bare on the earth. Find a quiet place or put on headphones to listen to classical or relaxing instrumental music. Close your eyes or focus on something calming. Breathe in slowly through your nose and out through your mouth, and feel your breath expanding your diaphragm. You may want to place one hand on your heart and one on your stomach as you breathe.

As you become calm, invite God to be present with you in your grief. Continue to inhale slowly and envision the cleansing and refreshing power of God entering you. As you exhale, you might visualize your grief going back out into the broad expanse of God's amazing universe to be redeemed. You may want to focus on a favorite Scripture. You'll find other relevant Scriptures relating to grief in the appendix of this book.

Reflect on these questions:

1. What are the signs that your grief is piling up and you need to take some time to attend to your sorrow?

2. Where is a safe place to go where you can experience your grief? Is there a place where you can feel connected to the one you lost and where you can invite God to join you in your pain?

3. Review the Focus Scripture from Chapter Three (Hebrews 4:14-16). Why is it significant that you have Jesus in heaven as a high priest who understands you and intercedes for you?

4. What is the best time for you to intentionally grieve? After you decide, schedule time to confront your grief. In the early days, you may need to take some private time every few hours, go on an extended personal retreat in a peaceful and scenic area, or spend time with a close friend. But do whatever it takes, even if it means you have to ask someone to cover for you at work, take care of your children over a weekend, or whatever.

5. Who are your grief companions? People will probably come to mind first, but also consider pets, or maybe just you and God. Give it some thought. People have very different needs which may change with time. It is typical to withdraw in the early aftermath of a painful loss, but there should be eventual movement toward reconnection as time passes. We are designed to both endure grief and celebrate community.

CHAPTER 6

FORWARD MOVEMENT AND CONTINUING BONDS

There is a time for everything,
and a season for every activity under the heavens:
a time to be born and a time to die,
a time to plant and a time to uproot
a time to kill and a time to heal,
a time to tear down and a time to build,
a time to weep and a time to laugh,
a time to mourn and a time to dance,
a time to scatter stones and a time to gather them,
a time to embrace and a time to refrain from embracing,
a time to search and a time to give up,
a time to keep and a time to throw away,
a time to tear and a time to mend,
a time to be silent and a time to speak,
a time to love and a time to hate,
a time for war and a time for peace.

ECCLESIASTES 3:1-8

Grief Discovery

Healthy grievers understand that there are seasons in life, forward movement, and change. Life is about surrender.

Like it or not, life is about movement. We don't understand that when we're young; it's something most of us only see in retrospect. Maybe you remember Ol' What's-His-Name and that oath the two of you took back in kindergarten to be friends forever. You haven't seen that guy in 50 years. Why not? Because you both moved on. And how about that teenage crush that didn't work out and made you feel like you were going to die? Well, take a look at him now and thank God that you moved on and didn't marry him. (He's currently on wife #3.)

People, places, and things come and go in the wake of the motion of our lives. But with age we often lose our enthusiasm for any further motion. We begin to resist change. Still, most of the things we love involve some degree of necessary change. Some of us move to the upper Midwest because we're enthralled with the beauty of spring, summer, and fall. But then that place we love changes for a season, and we really don't love those long, frigid winters. Some move south to take advantage of the milder winters, but then they swelter through the sticky, humid days of summer. We rejoice when the motion of time brings the birth of that new grandbaby, yet we realize that the same movement is edging us closer to the difficulties of old age and death.

Yes, life is about movement—a movement that often brings tremendous joys…and occasionally, great sorrow. The loss of someone you love can feel like it rips your heart out of your chest and leaves you empty and broken. To make things worse, you can feel like no one understands the magnitude of your pain. Yet it has happened and it appears to be out of your control. But what can you do?

You keep moving.

Motion and Emotion

One of the most significant things I look for in grieving people is change. I look for changes in the frequency, intensity and duration of grief. One term that captures this well is "forward movement." September Vaudrey is a colleague in the field of grief work, and we discussed this concept in a video interview I did with her. She has written a touching book about the tragic death of her 19-year-old daughter following a car accident: *Colors of Goodbye: A Memoir of Holding On, Letting Go, and Reclaiming Joy in the Wake of Loss*. Despite the crushing sorrow she felt, she refused to remain stuck in her grief. She kept moving forward, and today is an example of hope and strength for many others struggling with grief.

All of life is about movement. If you think about it, we witness regular movement from darkness to light, cycles of the seasons, rotation of the earth and planets, flow of water and air, and the list goes on.

The human body is a masterpiece of various systems of movement working in sync with one another. Most of us are somewhat familiar with the circulatory system as the heart pumps blood to all areas of the body to sustain life and health. Fewer of us know much about the lymphatic system, which is complementary to the circulatory system. Lymph is a fluid that also circulates throughout the body to protect it from illness by maintaining body fluid levels, absorbing digestive tract fats, producing antibodies that protect us from infection and disease, and more.

But before this chapter becomes an anatomy lesson, here's my point: The lymphatic system doesn't have a pump equivalent to the heart to move lymph to the appropriate organs and areas where it needs to be. Exercise and movement are essential for moving fluid through the system to the hundreds of lymph nodes throughout the body. When there are problems, those areas can become sensitive to touch and a source of pain, signaling that something is wrong. In addition to exercise and movement, other ways to keep lymph moving properly include gentle stretching and massage techniques, weight control, and avoiding unnecessary exposure to harmful chemicals that can get lodged in the system and cause problems.

I see the lymphatic system as a meaningful metaphor for how grief can get "stuck" as well. Grief is natural and normal. No one is immune to it. But grief is not healthy if we allow it to weigh us down indefinitely and do nothing about it. Do you tend to hold your grief? Or are you "exercising"—trying to process it so that it flows through you? We must do the necessary work to facilitate growth in our grieving. Through this workbook, I challenge you to do grief work to exercise the emotional aspects of your head, heart, body, and soul.

In Chapter Three we compared head grievers with heart grievers. Now we need to consider the body as well. Traumatologists have discovered that trauma is often held in the body, even when the brain doesn't acknowledge it. Grief can be held in the body as well. In fact, it is very common for people to come down with illness, colds, and other physical symptoms after experiencing a loss. They go to the doctor for physical symptoms, and doctors often don't take the time to ask a few questions to determine if the problem might be related to grief, which can compromise the immune system. Your grief may manifest itself physically in your body.

We tend to see the traumatic events of our lives as landmarks, or time stamps in our memories. I worked with people at the World Trade Center and family assistance center after the national tragedy on September 11, 2001. That event was a life-stopping, world-changing event for them, and they will forever reference their lives as pre-9/11 or post-9/11. More recently, we've all just gone through the worldwide coronavirus pandemic, and you'll overhear people talking about "before the pandemic" or "since the pandemic" to establish a time. Similarly, sorrow and grief do the same thing on individual levels. When families get together, they hardly need to refer to dates. Instead, they'll say, "That was the year Dad died, or "That's just before Mom had her stroke," or "It was shortly after

Uncle Bill was blinded in that accident." Much of life is perceived in terms of pre- or post-tragedy, pre- or post-loss.

Years ago I was one of the divorce group leaders and teachers at a megachurch. (Church leaders had wanted me to help lead the grief and trauma groups, but I was looking for a change from my everyday job. Besides, think of all the grief and trauma involved in divorce!) The participants were divided into groups of six people per table for the six-week sessions, and most groups had a good mix of perspectives: recently divorced, long-divorced, and a few who had just had a spouse ask for a divorce. But after a year, one of the senior leaders decided to divide the groups differently. He wanted to put all the people in the early impact phase, which he called the "raw people," in one group, and all those who had been divorced for years would be in another group. I told him I didn't think it was a good idea. He basically told me they were going to do it anyway, so I made it clear I was not taking the raw group. It was a good decision because the new groupings were a disaster. Why? The "raw people" had very little to offer one another because they were all in a very similar state of hopelessness and lack of direction. They could have used some real-life advice and mentoring from people who had been there. And the ones who were farther along at various levels of the healing process could have really benefited to see the raw people and realize how far they had come since they had been in that group.

I want to challenge you to carefully consider who you're spending time with. Grievers often feel a connection with others in grief who get their pain. However, you also need to make sure to spend time with others who are farther down the road and can inspire you to keep moving that direction. That truth is expressed beautifully in this poem:

Along the Road
Robert Browning Hamilton

I walked a mile with Pleasure,
She chattered all the way;
But left me none the wiser,
For all she had to say.
I walked a mile with Sorrow
And ne'er a word said she;
But, oh, the things I learned from her
When Sorrow walked with me![7]

In the early aftermath of loss, most people tend to see only challenges—the things they perceive as negative aspects of the loss. Yet as time goes on, your perspective should change. You will view life, people, yourself, your career, relationships, goals, and even God differently. You can eventually learn to deprioritize your pain and struggle and begin to treasure every day and every moment you have with those still in your life.

Continuing Bonds

One of the struggles for many grievers is the fear of forgetting essential aspects of their loved one's life and personality. The challenge is learning how to retain positive memories and remain connected to the one you loved without diminishing the love and admiration you have for those still living. You need to essentially reprioritize your emotions—letting go of the one you can no longer interact with and affirming your gratitude and appreciation for those you *can*. It can't be the same, but just because it's different doesn't mean it's wrong. In fact, it might be inappropriate to refuse to let go of a departed loved one.

Pam, one of my employees, was very close to her mother who lived with Pam and her husband before she died. One of their regular rituals was watching one of their favorite shows together. After her mother died, Pam and her husband were sitting on the couch together as that particular show was about to start. Pam said, "Oh, wait!" She got up, ran out of the room, and came back with her mother's urn, which she set between them on the couch. Her husband was totally freaked out. He called me the next day and said, "You have to help me with Pam. We have a situation!" The next day the three of us had a little talk. I started by saying, "I hear Momma watched the show with you last night." Pam laughed and said her husband had been more than a little startled by her action. We talked for a while and I explained that maybe there were other ways Pam could feel close to her mom the next time she and her husband watched the show together. As we explored some options, she decided that she could wear one of her mother's sweaters or another piece of her clothing…instead of putting the ashes of her mother between her and her husband.

After my father died, I literally walked in his shoes for months. We had the same shoe size and this helped me to feel close to him. He also had a rocking chair I had made for him in high school shop class that he used in his study when he studied and prayed. Whenever I sat in that chair during my prayer time, I felt closer to him and to God, and I felt grateful for all the prayers he had said for me through the years.

The former prominent perspective on grief originated from Sigmund Freud's work, *Mourning and Melancholia*. He promoted the belief that the bereaved must relinquish/disconnect attachment to the deceased to move forward. More current research, however, indicates that the goal of grief work should not be detachment, but rather *adaptation*—repositioning the lost loved one in what is called a "continuing bond."

It is important to note that adaptation must include lifestyle, habits, and routines. For instance, you shouldn't prepare the same amount of food you did when there were two of you. You may have to learn to handle additional household duties or hire someone to do those things. And you have to become accustomed to the fact that your loved one is no longer there to greet you at the door or come to bed with you at night.

When I was working with the Japanese survivors after their great earthquake and tsunami, I found that they were very intentional about trying to remember those who had died. They would often create a little shrine area in their house, or sometimes on the street, where they could pause to remember and honor those who had passed on.

Clinical psychologist Therese Rando defines two conditions for a healthy continuing bond with the deceased: (1) Recognizing that the person is dead and the implications of that; and (2) The bond must not interfere with moving forward into a new life.[7] In many of the situations where I find grievers are stuck in their grief, one or both of these conditions are not met.

Psychoanalyst John Bowlby identified healthy mourning as occurring when a griever accepts "both that a change has occurred in his external world and he is required to make corresponding changes in his internal, representational world and reorganize and perhaps reorient, his attachment behavior accordingly."[8]

C.S. Lewis wrote extensively on his experience of grieving the death of his wife. He talked about grasping and holding on to memories of her, but explains that it was only letting go that brought recovery and renewed memories. He states that when he mourned her the least, he "remembered her the best...and the remarkable thing is that since I stopped bothering about it, she seems to meet me everywhere."[9]

Christians should never view death as the final chapter for anyone. We believe the afterlife promises far greater joy and peace for a believing loved one than he or she ever experienced on earth, and that thought should provide comfort for those of us left behind. We are challenged not to grieve as those who have no hope (1 Thessalonians 4:13). Although we have a finite biological existence here on this earth, we believe the soul lives on at a higher level of existence with God.

My father has been dead for over ten years now, but I still feel very connected to him at times: when I read some of his books, sit in his chair, or visit places we went together. It's common for those who grieve to have experiences of feeling connected to their loved ones after death. They may have vivid dreams or visions, or they sense the person's presence in the room. Sometimes they feel like God gives them a sign through something like a bird or butterfly, or something that was meaningful to that person. Not everyone experiences things like this, but many do. When I discuss this phenomenon in my grief workshops, people frequently tell me their own stories. They often thank me because they "feel weird" talking about this to others. They're afraid people won't believe them or "think they're crazy."

Pause for a few moments to stop and reflect on what we have discussed in this chapter. Assess how your own experience conforms to the goals and guidelines listed below. Are you making changes? Is there forward movement? How so? Discuss your progress (or lack of it) with someone.

According to bereavement scientists, the most healthy grievers have the following things in common:

> They are less likely to use avoidance and distraction as coping strategies.

> They understand that waves of grief will come episodically and are willing to confront a full range of emotions.

> They find comfort in talking about or thinking about the deceased. This brings them feelings of happiness, joy, and peace.

> They understand that happiness and sadness are both normal.

> They realize that it is common to have continuing bonds with the deceased, but that their relationship priorities must change.

Also take some time to reflect on the following:

1. What are some intentional things you can do to keep the memory of your departed loved one alive?

2. When do you feel closest to him or her?

3. What can you do to let the person go and reposition him or her in a different place in your life...all while holding on to cherished memories?

CHAPTER 7

WHEN IT DOESN'T GET BETTER

Therefore, since we are surrounded by such a great cloud of witnesses, let us throw off everything that hinders and the sin that so easily entangles. And let us run with perseverance the race marked out for us, fixing our eyes on Jesus, the pioneer and perfecter of faith. For the joy set before him he endured the cross, scorning its shame, and sat down at the right hand of the throne of God. Consider him who endured such opposition from sinners, so that you will not grow weary and lose heart.

HEBREWS 12:1-3

Grief Discovery:

Healthy grievers are intentional about assessing their emotional, spiritual, and relational growth and getting the feedback of trusted others.

I once worked with a woman who was experiencing immense grief after finding out her husband was having an affair. He had immediately ended the affair and couple was working faithfully to restore their marriage. For quite some time they appeared to be doing very well. But about nine months later the woman again started feeling extreme levels of grief and overreacting to things her husband said and did. They couldn't figure out why she was regressing after the relationship had been going so well for so long. As I explored this with her, I realized she had just hit the one-year anniversary of the time she found out about the affair. Sometimes our bodies remember when our minds don't. I have observed this phenomenon frequently with people through the years and have found that it is important for people to prepare for such times.

Many other things can trigger a grief upsurge, including seeing someone who reminds you of the departed person, going back to a place the two of you used to frequent, or hearing a certain song. Smells are some of the strongest triggers. Certain scents can trigger a part of the brain, and your memory will take you instantly back to another place and time. For years after my work following 9/11, I conscientiously attempted to avoid any flowers that smelled like the ones most often used at funeral homes, and any type of plastic that smelled like a body bag. However, other scents can trigger *positive* memories, so you can make your brain work for you as well. One man whose children had died in an accident placed some of their clothing items in sealed plastic bags so he could retain their smells.

When Trauma Is Associated with Loss

Whenever trauma is associated with loss, you may need to seek professional help because there are some great ways to help resolve trauma. Some people find Eye Movement Desensitization and Reprocessing (EMDR) helpful. When I work with such people, I use horses on our ranch combined with prayer, meditation, and psychosensory techniques that are very effective.

In the Focus Scripture for this chapter, the apostle Paul talks about running a race. We need to keep our focus on Christ as we progress toward the finish line, regardless of how fast we're going. The problem for many of us, however, is that we tend to keep watching the others around us, see how they are doing, and then judge ourselves by them. That is a recipe for failure. Everyone is different. We have different personalities, losses, experiences, and reactions. We struggle with different issues and in different ways. However, I fully believe that each of us has much to learn, and your journey toward healing can be just as unique and profound as anyone's.

The question should never be, "Am I making progress fast enough?" Instead, the bottom line is, "Am I experiencing regular forward movement in my grief?" Here's the reality: some days you will feel like you're really making progress and other days you won't. That was the purpose of the exercise in Chapter Five where you defined your grief journey, to identify what you experienced during each leg of your journey. Sometimes grievers are surprised to encounter a setback after an extended period of doing much better. Grief has its emotional highs and lows. You can't always control what emotions you feel, so instead of judging them, stop to assess what might be going on.

Take some time to reflect on your grief triggers. When you identify what triggers affect you most, you can prepare for them going forward. Consider the following potential triggers.

> *Dates*
> When did the loss occur? You may want to mark your calendar a few weeks before the date to emotionally prepare for potential flashbacks of memory. You can plan to be with a friend or family member that day if you anticipate it being too hard to be alone.

> *Smells*
> Have you ever connected any scents to traumatic memories of your loss? Common triggers include clothing scents, perfumes, hospital smells, diesel fumes, certain foods, etc.

> *Visuals*
> Do any visual cues ever trigger unexpected memories? These could include things like shapes, colors, movement, speed, etc.

> *Sounds*
> How about sounds that trigger responses from you? People frequently struggle with noises like screams, gunshots, and police or ambulance sirens.

If you find yourself unexpectedly thinking about a painful loss that you thought you had sufficiently recovered from, stop and see if you can detect what is prompting the memory. Did you just smell something? Hear something? See something? By creating an awareness of your triggers, you can then work to find something to help dissipate them. Don't just try to stuff them down and keep going. Sometimes you may need to put it out of your thoughts for a period of time, but make sure you stop to deal with it at some point.

If you are driving and become overwhelmed with grief to the point that you are tearing up, pull off the road in a safe place and allow yourself to cry. If you are in a meeting and find yourself suddenly at the mercy of one of your triggers, excuse yourself, go compose yourself, and return. Just give yourself enough time to recall what was triggered, identify the emotion that is there, and allow yourself to experience it.

Listen to What Others Are Saying

One of my seminary professors told my class something I've never forgotten. I use it with my clients a lot. He said, "If one person calls you an ass, take note, but you may ignore it. If two people call you an ass, pay closer attention. If three people call you an ass, buy a saddle!"

People deep in grief often don't have a clear perspective of themselves or the world around them. It's important to listen to trustworthy people who care about you to get an objective opinion as to how they think you're doing. But be sure to use discernment in deciding whom to listen to. Not everyone understands grief, and you don't want to base your assessment on one person's ignorance. We all have friends who think you should be back to your old self in a week or so, regardless of what you've been through. Hopefully, through this book, you're developing a better understanding of what healthy grieving looks like so you will know better.

Healing from loss takes time, so take it! Be gentle with yourself, but also be cautious because grief can propel you to growth or it can drag you down a path of destruction. It's your choice, but not always a simple one. It's easy to descend into an emotional quagmire that you're not aware you've sunk into. This is especially true if you have vulnerabilities from your past, such as drugs, alcohol, or eating disorders. If your family of origin struggled with any of these issues, beware! It's tempting to start self-medicating with food or some ill-advised substance trying to regain a state of balance.

It is common—and healthy—to withdraw for a while after loss, yet it is important to reconnect and re-enter the world before too much time passes. One big warning sign is a continual reluctance to re-engage with life and other people.

I was working with a veteran who had PTSD and who had experienced a lot of losses and grief from his personal life and military career. In one of our sessions he told me, "My sister thinks I'm an ass, but I really just have PTSD." That prompted a lengthy discussion where I was eventually able to help him understand that it's possible for someone to have PTSD and *not* "be an ass."

Take some time now to think about your recent interactions with other people.

1. Has anyone told you (or perhaps strongly hinted) that they are worried about you? If so, do you trust this person's opinion? Why or why not?

2. What are some other things that people have told you, hoping to be helpful? Have you found yourself arguing with anyone? Can you detect any connection between your grief and your ability to get along with others?

3. When people express concern for you, do you ask them why? Or do you try to change the subject?

You really can't stop grief. It will come out one way or another, but you have a choice in how you mourn your loss. You can grieve in a healthy or unhealthy way. So when you have trustworthy people who are trying to be supportive, see what you can learn from them. They may see something you don't. Even if you think they're wrong, don't argue with them. You want to make sure you are not descending into a negative place. If you refuse to acknowledge and deal with your grief, it has a way of coming out sideways in the most inappropriate ways and times.

Stubborn Forms of Grief

I have worked a lot in African-American communities. I remember the first Black funeral I attended. The family members were accompanied by women all dressed in white, with fans in their hands. When I asked about them, my friend explained that it was "for when people fall out." I soon saw that strong outward expressions of grief can take a physical toll, and people may even faint. At this funeral I witnessed an intense verbal and physical way to grieve.

About a month later I attended another funeral with a Black family from the same community, and it was a totally different experience. The family at this funeral demonstrated a much calmer and more composed expression of grief. Neither method of grieving was better or worse than the other. People experience grief and express it very differently in their styles of mourning. Not all people grieve the same way.

But regardless how we deal with grief, sometimes it just doesn't seem to get better. You may hear various clinical terms to define this inability to get beyond your grief and move on. I personally prefer either "prolonged grief" or "complicated grief" because I think both terms capture the essence of the problem. Grief is complicated and takes time to heal. The more complicated the loss, and the more losses that are involved within a time frame, the more a griever may struggle.

Grief can contribute to behaviors that may lead to a disorder, but grief begins as a normal response to loss before it sometimes is complicated by other factors. Cultural and religious influences, for example, vary broadly from one person and group to another. What would seem to be quite normal in one setting may seem very abnormal in another.

Prolonged Grief

Prolonged grief disorder is the newest disorder added to the Diagnostic and Statistical Manual of Mental Disorders (DSM) in 2022. Think of this manual as the bible for mental health clinicians. It's what they use when assigning a diagnosis to enable a patient to receive insurance reimbursement.

The American Psychological Association (APA) lists some symptoms of prolonged grief disorder. They clarify that grief is a natural response to the loss of a loved one, and for most people, the symptoms of grief should decrease over time. However, among a small group of people, the feeling of intense grief persists, and the symptoms become severe enough to cause problems that stop them from continuing with their lives. The intense and persistent grief these people experience is disabling and affects everyday functioning in a way that typical grieving does not. If it has been more than a year since your loss, you might consider seeking help from a mental health professional if you feel your condition has stayed the same or is getting steadily worse.

Below are some of the indicators of prolonged grief disorder (specifically, after the death of a loved one). Determine to what extent each one applies to you on a scale of 1 (not at all) to 10 (all the time), and note your rating beside each one. If you're preparing to discuss this with a mental health professional, make notes of what you are experiencing. Be sure to indicate any positive changes as well as your prolonged struggles.

_____Identity disruption (such as feeling as though part of yourself has died)

_____Marked sense of disbelief about the death

_____Avoidance of reminders that the person is dead

_____Intense emotional pain (such as anger, bitterness, sorrow) related to the death

_____Difficulty with reintegration (such as problems engaging with friends, pursuing interests, planning for the future)

_____Emotional numbness (absence or marked reduction of emotional experience)

_____Feeling that life is meaningless

_____Intense loneliness (feeling alone or detached from others)

What does this exercise tell you about how you've processed grief so far?

Complicated Grief

Think of complicated grief as a chronic, heightened state of mourning that doesn't seem to dissipate. Columbia University currently offers a helpful five-question inventory that you can take through their Center for Prolonged Grief. (On their site they alter between the terms "complicated grief" and "prolonged grief" because both terms are currently in flux. And because internet addresses are prone to change, I won't provide a link, but you can do an internet search and find it quickly.) I frequently have my clients take this inventory at different intervals to see how they are progressing. I recently spoke with someone who had just taken it, and then I had her retake it as she would have answered it six months ago. It was very helpful for her to look back and realize that her scores had lowered dramatically. It was a good indicator of forward movement that she hadn't been aware of, and a special encouragement during her "hard days."

In the same way you rated prolonged grief symptoms, use the same 1 to 10 scale for this detailed list of key indicators of complicated grief.

_____ Extreme focus on the loss and reminders of the loved one

_____ Intense longing or pining for the deceased

_____ Problems accepting the death

_____ Numbness or detachment

_____ Preoccupation with your sorrow

_____ Bitterness about your loss

_____ Inability to enjoy life

_____ Depression or deep sadness

_____ Trouble carrying out normal routines

_____ Withdrawing from social activities

_____ Feeling that life holds no meaning or purpose

_____ Irritability or agitation

_____ Lack of trust in others

_____ Keeping the yearning process alive through your habits

_____ Creating shrines for the deceased

_____ Constantly talking about the deceased or looking at his or her picture

_____ Refusal to permit space in your life for anything except memories of your lost loved one

_____ A level of devotion to the memories of the deceased that approaches addiction

_____ Remembrance of the past and anticipation of the future through a lens of distressed yearning for the deceased

_____ Hopelessness about the future

_____ Intense and unabating waves of painful emotion

_____ Preoccupation with memories that make it difficult to recall past (or envision future) events that do not include the deceased loved one

_____ Ongoing focus on significant past life events when the deceased was alive

_____ Fantasies about what the future might hold if the deceased loved one was still alive

What does this exercise tell you about how your grief has been complicated?

After the loss of a loved one, the remaining spouse or friend or family often feel they can't or shouldn't allow themselves to get better. Do you ever feel guilty when you have a good day, experience joy, or have fun?

Think of it this way: What if *you* had been the one who died? Would you want your spouse, family, and friends to live the rest of their lives in deep mourning? Would you want them to honor your memory by refusing to try to get better, never experiencing joy again, and never finding a new sense of meaning and purpose in life?

I hope your answer is no. You would want your loved one to grieve your death and miss you, certainly, but eventually you would want them to create a happy and productive life. So don't beat yourself up on days you feel better!

If your answer was yes, you probably have other issues you need to address, which almost certainly is part of the reason you're not getting better! I often find that when people are stuck in their grief, it's because of an unresolved issue in the relationship. Maybe you had a big argument shortly before the person died, or you failed to honor something you'd promised, or you had somehow mistreated or offended the person and had never asked for forgiveness—the list goes on. No one is perfect and every relationship has issues. It's too late to correct past mistakes, but beating yourself up for the rest of your life doesn't do anyone any good.

Can you identify any such lingering issues in your past relationship? If so, list anything below that you think may be keeping you stuck in your grief.

Next, you need to think about what you can do to resolve these issues. You may be able to work through them alone, but don't hesitate to call on a friend, a grief coach, or some clinical help to move forward. I frequently do exercises with people to help them release past regrets and find freedom for the future.

I cover this topic more in-depth in the *Grief Factor* book, but I want to briefly mention how the brain impacts our grief. Research shows that when people get stuck in complicated grief, a part of the brain called the *nucleus accumbens* responds by secreting dopamine. This region of the brain is a neural interface that regulates motivation, action, and reward. People with more complicated levels of grief have higher levels of activity, resulting in unabating levels of yearning, desiring, and longing for that which was lost, associated with the constant desire to see the departed person again. Grievers can get stuck in a cycle where they obsess over aspects of the loss. But like a drug habit, it doesn't bring them long-term pleasure or satisfaction. They keep obsessing about the loss but don't end up feeling better. It's a vicious cycle that interferes with adapting to the loss and moving forward.

Therese Rando offers another warning for those struggling with complicated grief. She says you shouldn't expect to grieve a loss the same way you grieved a similar loss ten years ago. You have changed, as have many other factors since then.

> In brief, the demarcation between uncomplicated and complicated mourning is hazy at best and constantly changing. Such change is due not only to advancements in data collection in this area but also to the fact that no determination of abnormality can be made without taking into consideration the various sets of factors known to influence any response to loss. Reactions to loss can only be interpreted within the context of factors that circumscribe the particular loss for the particular mourner in the particular circumstances in which the loss took place.[10]

Holding On and Letting Go

Life is about movement, and so is grieving. The challenge of maintaining your forward motion is to learn what you need to leave behind and what to continue to hold tightly. Many of us benefit from assessment and work in this process.

As the book of Job opens, we see Job lose essentially everything he has at one time. He loses all his children, all his servants, and all his possessions in a single day. First consider how you would feel if that happened to you. Then take a look at Job's response:

> Then Job stood up, tore his robe, shaved his head, fell to the ground, bowed very low, and exclaimed:

> "I left my mother's womb naked,
>   and I will return to God naked.
> The Lord has given,
>   and the Lord has taken.
> May the name of the Lord be blessed."
>   Job neither sinned nor charged God with wrongdoing in all of this.
>   (Job 1:20-22 ISV)

This passage provides three important insights:

First, *Job's grief response.*

Despite the suddenness and magnitude of Job's loss, we see him in a state of surrender. If anyone deserved to give up on life and wallow in grief, it was Job. (Indeed, the advice of his wife would be, "Curse God and die!" [Job 2:9]) Job would certainly struggle with the why-me's and what-nows that we all do, but he starts with a positive mindset.

Second, *Job's objective assessment.*

No sooner had Job lost everything than he realized that none of those things were his to begin with. He came into the world with nothing and wouldn't take anything with him when he died. Rather than complain about his great loss, he gave praise to God for what he'd *had*.

And third, *Job's refusal to assign blame.*

Think of what a shock this must have been, yet "Job neither sinned nor charged God with wrongdoing." The rest of the book of Job details Job's search for answers and explanations for what had happened. But wow, how many of us can so quickly leave our pains and frustrations in God's hands after a personal disaster? We may get there eventually, but most of us first go through a prolonged period of lament and attempts to blame someone (often God).

Working through your grief is about forward movement. As a griever you need to understand the importance of allowing grief to flow *through* you until you can eventually release it. When grief gets stuck in the body and mind, it *will* cause problems.

After you've given serious thought to what you can learn from Job's examples, we'll close out this chapter with three New Testament insights. They're all derived from a short and sweet challenge from the Apostle Paul to the church in Thessalonica (and by extension, to you and me).

Here's his exhortation:

> Examine everything;
>> hold firmly to that which is good,
>>> abstain from every form of evil.
>>>> (1 Thessalonians 5:21-22)

Let's consider what Paul is asking us to do by applying each of these challenges to our effort to move on after we tend to get bogged down in grief.

Examine Everything!

Great loss has a way of shaking us to our foundation, but if we paid more attention to nature, we might not be so troubled by that. This whole world is regularly being shaken and shaped by the forces of nature. Earthquakes deep underground move the surface of the earth, creating spectacular landforms and scenic views. Volcanoes spew hot lava up through the earth to create new landmasses. Wildfires rage through fields and woods, but their initial destruction creates a foundation for strong new growth.

In the aftermath of these events, tourists spend lots of money and travel many miles to view the beauty of these disasters that, in God's design, have been recovered and rebuilt. Yellowstone is essentially a perpetually simmering volcano just beneath the earth's surface, providing all sorts of fascinating natural wonders. The Grand Canyon is the result of centuries of erosion. Pick your favorite island paradise, and it's the result of former turbulence that caused underwater mountains to spring up. Beauty now exists where chaos once reigned.

Natural disasters can appear frightening and insurmountable at the time, yet in the long run, nature creates a beautiful result from them. Similarly, personal disasters—especially trauma and loss—have a way of making us look at the world, life, and others in very different ways. You shouldn't be bothered when you see you aren't functioning at the same level during times of great grief. This is all by divine design. The experience provides an opportunity to slow down, attend to your grief, and begin to rebuild your strength from your core outward. As the shock wears off, you start to slowly recover and assess your losses.

In this chapter we are focusing on the later movement of grief, still moving forward, as we start putting things back together and rebuilding our lives. Like the aftermath of a natural disaster, it can be slow and messy. But remember that you're in it for the long run. The longer you keep moving forward, the better the scenery will look.

A catastrophic magnitude 7.0 earthquake struck Haiti in January 2010. The epicenter was 16 miles west of Port-au-Prince, the capital city. Overnight 30,000 people moved into a former soccer arena next to The Salvation Army headquarters. While working that disaster, I heard many stories from survivors of how they didn't feel safe for a long time afterward. Even when their houses were still standing, a lot of people feared aftershocks and refused to return home until they felt the risk was over. And even when they were told that their house was assessed as safe, some still didn't want to return.

After sustaining life and caring for the needs of survivors, one of the first tasks of emergency management following a widespread disaster is to carefully assess the damage. The same goes for personal crises. As the Apostle Paul said, "Examine everything." To be clear, he was talking about the danger of false teachings making their way into the church. But I think a thorough examination is just as necessary when false perceptions or beliefs about the loss of your loved one prevent you from grieving properly and then moving forward. Let's see more precisely who and what you should examine.

Examine Yourself and Your Beliefs

A proper examination requires time alone to hear God, get a good handle on your emotions, and process your loss. You can't do this with the clamor and nonstop pace of the world rushing by, which is why I often urge people to explore different ways to mourn their loss. Many choose to go to the ocean, a quiet farm, the mountains, or a wilderness area—someplace to provide renewal and a safe distance from the burdens of their past. This can be an amazing time of rest, reconnection, and healing.

Examine What Others Tell You

We are designed to sometimes be alone and reap the many benefits of peace and solitude. Yet we're not to retreat from the world *permanently*, because we are also designed to be with others who can love and support us. As we've seen, we often don't think clearly in times of sorrow because we can develop a very distorted view of the world. It is easy to make rash decisions that we later regret. The situation will most likely look very different a year after the loss. In the meantime, we need trusted and wise people as companions and sounding boards.

The following Scriptures advise us to examine the sources of feedback.

> Beloved, do not believe every spirit, but test the spirits to see whether they are from God, for many false prophets have gone out into the world. (1 John 4:1 ESV)

> For the time is coming when people will not endure sound teaching, but having itching ears they will accumulate for themselves teachers to suit their own passions, and will turn away from listening to the truth and wander off into myths. (2 Timothy 4:3-4 ESV)

> Then we will no longer be infants, tossed back and forth by the waves, and blown here and there by every wind of teaching and by the cunning and craftiness of people in their deceitful scheming. (Ephesians 4:14)

Hold Firmly to That Which Is Good

This second exhortation from the Apostle Paul is really two instructions. The first challenge we have is to determine what things are good. When we're thinking straight, we might hear that and think "How obvious!" But when we are hurt, angry, and in the midst of grieving, we can temporarily lose our moral compass and ability to discern what things are good for us…much less which of those things are best. When we admit the fuzziness of our perceptions and trust the advice and guidance of trusted friends, we aren't likely to "throw the baby out with the bathwater," as they say.

Then, after we are satisfied that we've found something good to hold on to—whether a ray of hope for a better future, confidence that we're going to somehow weather this storm, the support of friends and family, or whatever—hold on to those things with a vise grip. Let go of whatever is holding you back, but squeeze tightly when you find a lifeline that helps you get farther along your journey.

I like the way Richard Rohr expresses this concept: "All great spirituality is about letting go. It trains us in both detachment and attachment: detachment from the passing so we can attach to the substantial."[11]

Protective Boundaries

As we talk about holding on and letting go, let's consider the boundaries and the protective systems around us. When we are in deep grief, we become more vulnerable. We need protection from others and things that can be harmful to us. But we're also trying to get stronger, so we don't want to be smothered by overprotection. Grievers often struggle with helping those around them understand their needs while simultaneously providing an *appropriate* amount of protection for themselves.

Healthy boundaries protect you from harm, but allow good to come through. Think about your skin, a semipermeable membrane covering your body. Blood is circulating and all sorts of biological systems and organs are endlessly working just beneath the skin's protective covering, yet it can breathe and absorb vitamin D. Your skin allows heat and sweat to leave the body, but prevents rain and bathwater from getting in. Skin is a classic example of a healthy boundary.

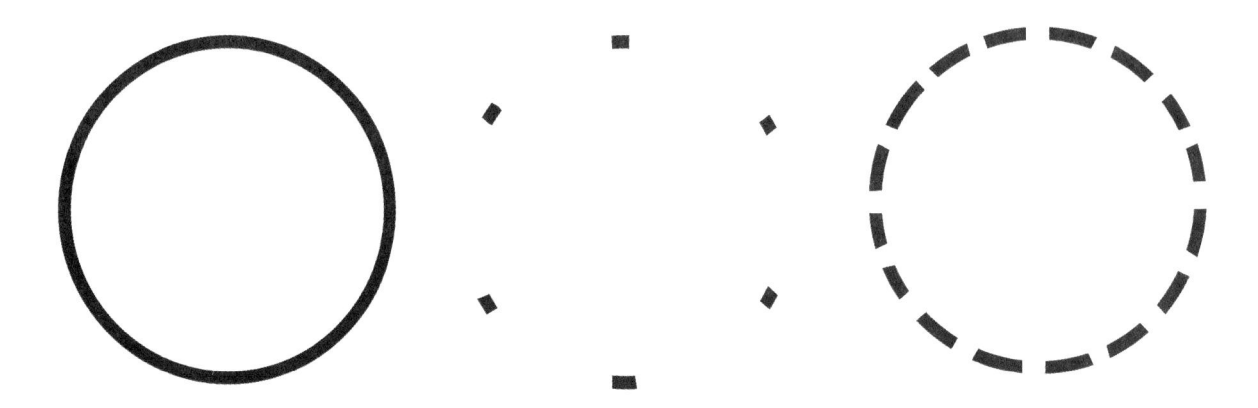

Consider the three boundary diagrams above.[12] Think of them as a depiction of different models of family systems. I have worked with all three types of systems through the years.

Overprotective and rigid boundary system

The model on the left is thick and rigid, and doesn't allow anything to go in or out of it—including any kind of positive input. In this type of system, people often feel restricted. Some may desire such a high degree of protection at times, but most would feel excessively controlled.

Unprotected and vulnerable no-boundary system

The center model is the opposite of the first one. It has huge gaps in it and does not provide adequate protection. In a family model like this one, people often don't feel cared for or protected. With so much "freedom," they often don't feel safe. They crave more structure.

A healthy boundary system

The model on the right depicts a more healthy balance within a system. This is a semipermeable system, flexible and adaptable. It maintains a protective barrier to keep those within from outside harm or danger, but will open up to admit anything good and helpful.

Abstain from Every Form of Evil

Paul closes his short list of exhortations with a plea for us to purge all evil from our thoughts and actions. When people are working through their grief but not seeing forward movement and growth, they often hold on to things they need to let go of, or engage in things that are not helpful. Again, they may need the assistance of others to see if they could be harboring emotions like anger, unforgiveness, and bitterness. They may be allowing their emotions to control them, instead of vice versa.

Scripture repeatedly reminds us to renew our minds, to focus our eyes on Christ, and to forgive. We are not perfect, nor are we expected to be. When we mess up and sin—and we will!—repentance and course correction will put us back on the path back to personal contentment, healthy relationships, and peace.

1. Has the content of this chapter given you workable ideas to try when you feel that you're stalled and just not getting any better? Which one(s), specifically?

2. Can you relate to any of the lessons from Job's life or the challenges of the Apostle Paul? If so, which ones? And in what ways?

3. Which of the boundary perimeters do you feel best illustrates your personal life right now?

4. What kind of boundary did you have before your loss? While growing up in your family of origin?

5. Is your boundary system consistent, or does it vary when you're at work? At church? With your family? With close friends?

CHAPTER 8

SO NOW WHAT? SPIRITUAL DIMENSIONS OF GRIEF

I am worn out from my groaning. All night long I flood my bed with weeping and drench my couch with tears.

PSALM 6:6

Grief Discovery

Healthy grievers are real with their emotional and spiritual struggles with God and others.

The writings of C.S. Lewis have inspired readers for decades now—children and adults alike. His *Mere Christianity* has provided new insights that guided countless people to a much richer understanding of God. Having remained an agnostic for much of his life prior to his conversion, he understood the frustration of trying to understand the mysteries of the Christian faith—particularly the nature of God. Lewis's honesty was quite brazen at times, even shocking to some. But when he described his personal experience with grief, it was something that grievers could really relate to. After his wife died tragically, he struggled as we all do with questions about God. Here's what he wrote:

> No one ever told me that grief felt so like fear. I am not afraid, but the sensation is like being afraid. The same fluttering in the stomach, the same restlessness, the yawning. I keep on swallowing.

> At other times it feels like being mildly drunk, or concussed. There is a sort of invisible blanket between the world and me. I find it hard to take in what anyone says. Or perhaps, hard to want to take it in. It is so uninteresting. Yet I want the others to be about me. I dread the moments when the house is empty. If only they would talk to one another and not me….
>
> Meanwhile, where is God? This is one of the most disquieting symptoms. When you are happy, so happy that you have no sense of needing Him, so happy that you are tempted to feel His claims upon you as an interruption, if you remember yourself and turn to Him with gratitude and praise, you will be—or so it feels—welcomed with open arms. But go to Him when your need is desperate, when all other help is vain, and what do you find? A door slammed in your face, and a sound of bolting and double bolting on the inside. After that, silence….
>
> Not that I am (I think) in much danger of ceasing to believe in God. The real danger is of coming to believe such dreadful things about Him. The conclusion I dread is not 'So there's no God after all', but 'So this is what God's really like. Deceive yourself no longer.'"[13]

Have you ever tried to get God's attention and felt as if he slammed the door in your face and then double bolted it? And if so, do you tend to share that experience with lots of other people? Or are you concerned with what they might think of you if you made such a statement?

C.S. Lewis struggled, as so many of us do, with reconciling a view of God as good, faithful, powerful, and actively involved in the world during periods when we're confronted with so much adversity and suffering. If that includes you, you are not alone!

Grief has the potential to totally change your faith. Some go through what we often term a "crisis of faith." Such times have the power to shake us out of our naïve and innocent pre-loss state and force us to wrestle with harsh realities at a level we never previously encountered. It can feel terrifying to go into uncharted waters, yet the result of going through those scary experiences is a more complete transformation into the image of God—the "you" that God created you to be. But be warned, because such a transformation gets messy at times! Bear in mind along the way that your doubts, struggles, fears, and even anger are normal. They're okay! Just keep moving ahead.

I intentionally saved the spiritual dimensions of grief to include in this closing chapter, for a number of reasons. I often say that grief camps far more frequently in the spiritual than the psychological realm, yet I am concerned because many of my clients do not feel that the church understands their grief. After trauma or loss we are forced to look at life, God, the world, and others through new eyes. The spiritual dimensions of grief require us to wrestle with loss at both a head and a heart level. If you're among the grievers who find that their churches do not provide a place for them to recover, my prayer is that you'll find a great small group or grief support group to guide you into a better understanding of grief and life.

The Power of Song

We may have lost the language of lament in many of our churches, but it's still throughout our Scriptures. From the first cries of lament after Abel's senseless murder of Cain (Genesis 4:10) to the pleas for justice from martyred saints in Revelation (6:9-11), godly people have lamented losses suffered from merciless and evil people. Lament is every bit as biblical as praise.

To offset some of the injustices imposed on them, early Christians were encouraged to sing "psalms and hymns and spiritual songs" (Ephesians 5:19). Paul and Silas sang hymns after being severely flogged and while imprisoned (Acts 16:25). Jesus and his disciples sang a hymn just before departing for Gethsemane, where he would soon be arrested and crucified (Matthew 26:30).

But the biggest biblical focus on spiritual songs by far is the book of Psalms. It's essentially an entire hymnal tucked right in the middle of the Old Testament, even though we've lost the accompanying melodies. And if you think C.S. Lewis went a bit far in questioning God during times of personal loss, just leaf through the Psalms sometime and look at some of the psalmists' comments and questions. Their cries should serve as comfort and strength to us as survivors, as they draw upon their experiences of praise, thanksgiving, and lament.

The psalms pulled ancient worshipers closer together during good times and bad. They sang for joy with "Songs of Ascents" (Psalms 120—134) as they traveled upward toward Jerusalem for regular celebrations, and they wrote psalms to describe their despair and homesickness while in exile in Babylon (Psalm 137). Jesus quoted the opening line of Psalm 22 as he was hanging on the cross. We can learn from such examples that when God appears distant or hidden, we can draw strength from the broader faith community. Scripture can be a sustaining force during times of suffering, and in the form of song, it can become even more powerful.

However, the melody must never diminish the message. I think the church often does a disservice to unbelievers and believers alike. Many people have turned away from Christianity because they feel that the always-upbeat message of love and grace is unrelated to the world of loss in which they live. Survivors who are seeking spiritual care and connection desire a faith that acknowledges the real-life pain they suffer every day in this far-from-perfect world. A church that focuses entirely on positive aspects of faith and sings only "happy, happy, joy songs" (as one of my clients once labeled them) has nothing to offer them, so they either find another church to try or leave the faith altogether. When in phases of deep grief, it's hard enough to get up and go to church to begin with. If people find no reason to return, they probably won't.

The Psalms of Lament

Anyone looking for relevant expressions of loss and confusion should find no shortage in Scripture—especially in the book of Psalms. The psalms are often divided into three categories: praise, thanksgiving, and lament. You might be surprised to discover that the lament psalms far outnumber the praise songs.

Laments are spontaneous prayers that express to God the pain and suffering that accompany trauma, crisis, death, and grief. The lament can be an appeal from an individual or entire community seeking deliverance from trouble and distress.

Most laments have three distinguishable subjects: God, the one expressing the lamentation, and the enemy or persecutor who is the instrumental source of grief. Laments are recorded for lots of different reasons, including:[14]

Sickness	Psalm 6
Public Slander	Psalm 31
False Legal Accusations	Psalms 35, 109
General Enmity	Psalms 3, 13, 54, 86
Poverty, Exploitation, and Oppression	Psalms 52, 53, 102
Consequences of Personal Sin	Psalm 51
National Distress, Including Enemy Siege	Psalm 83
Military Defeat	Psalms 74, 79, 80, 137
General Societal Evil	Psalms 10, 12, 82
Effects of Famine and Drought	Psalm 85

Throughout this book, references have been made to grief as a journey. Various laments refer to different stages of that journey. Walter Brueggemann designates three general groupings:

> - Psalms of Orientation (Creation; Wisdom; Retribution; Well-Being);
> - Psalms of Disorientation (Personal and Communal Laments); and
> - Psalms of New Orientation (Thanksgiving Songs; Hymns of Praise).[15]

Generally, these phases track with how most of us naturally progress through life, but as we encounter suffering and loss, we might at times move back and forth from one phase to another. Brueggemann offers an example of Jesus' progress from the description of him provided in Philippians 2:5-11:

Orientation: "Though he was in the form of God…."
Disorientation: "[He] emptied himself."
New Orientation: "Therefore God has highly exalted him…."

Take a moment to reflect on where *you* are right now. Are you more in a state of orientation, a state of disorientation, or a state of new orientation? Explain your answer.

Are you where you'd *like* to be? If not, what are your next steps to get there?

It does little good to only *talk about* psalms of lament. Let's take time here for a close-up look at one of them. I've chosen Psalm 13 because it's short, yet contains relevant themes for people undergoing a crisis. (Pay attention, because later I'll ask you to write your own psalm of lament.)

> ¹ How long, Lord? Will you forget me forever?
>   How long will you hide your face from me?
> ² How long must I wrestle with my thoughts
>   and day after day have sorrow in my heart?
>   How long will my enemy triumph over me?
> ³ Look on me and answer, Lord my God.
>   Give light to my eyes, or I will sleep in death,
> ⁴ and my enemy will say, "I have overcome him,"
>   and my foes will rejoice when I fall.
> ⁵ But I trust in your unfailing love;
>   my heart rejoices in your salvation.
> ⁶ I will sing the Lord's praise,
>   for he has been good to me.

To begin with, this psalm is one of many that is often attributed to David. We can't be entirely certain that David wrote all the ones credited to him, but if this is one of them, that means the author is the same David whose faith in God enabled him to single-handedly take down Goliath… the same warrior David who defeated all his enemies and united Israel and Judah into one great nation… the same spiritually committed David who was known as "a man after [God's] own heart" (Acts 13:22) and made every preparation for his son Solomon to build God's temple in Jerusalem. Yet here we see a David who, like the rest of us, has found himself in a situation beyond his control, wrestling with sorrow and confusion. No one goes unscathed forever from the awfulness of grief.

1. Anytime a name or phrase is repeated in a Bible passage, it usually means "Pay attention. This is important." What phrase do you see repeated in Psalm 13 (verses 1 and 2)?

2. What do you think is the significance of the repetition?

3. Notice, too, that this psalm contains no introduction or formal address. The writer's anguish is evident from the opening line. He doesn't bother with pleasantries or attempt to sugarcoat his situation, but launches immediately into the questions arising from the sorrow of his soul. What prompted the writing of this lament? What was amiss in his life? (v. 2)

The writer doesn't bother with details about his unnamed "enemy." As we've seen, his complaint is really with God … and he doesn't mind saying so! Lots of us are reluctant to let God know how we really feel—as if God won't find out unless we tell him. God knows our every thought, so the sooner we're honest with him, the sooner we're likely to find what we need for help and healing.

1. The psalmist's initial accusation was that God had forgotten him (v. 1). What does that suggest about his relationship with God prior to the writing of this lament?

2. The complaint against God intensifies in the next question, "How long will you hide your face from me? (v. 1) It's bad enough to think God may have *forgotten* you during times of crisis and sorrow, but to accuse him of *hiding* suggests an intentional act of neglect. It's not unlike C.S. Lewis's feeling that God had shut the door in his face and double-bolted the lock. These first two verses express great frustration, yet they also indicate a continued desire for God's presence with the psalmist in the midst of his pain. When have you felt both frustration at God and desire for His presence?

3. The psalmist clearly felt abandoned and forgotten, and his future must have seemed bleak because he added the word "forever." In the midst of deep pain it is not uncommon for people (even those who are strong in their faith) to feel invisible to others and to God. Have you ever felt like that? If so, when?

4. Yet even in his suffering, the writer isn't giving up on God. He didn't ask, "*Why* did you let this happen to me?" By asking "*How long* …?" he indicates that he's still awaiting a response. How is that confirmed in verses 3 and 4?

5. And then you'll notice an abrupt shift in focus between verses 1-4 and verses 5-6. It's as if the psalmist stops and takes a deep breath. What do you think was responsible for the sudden change?

6. We sometimes refer to people having a "change of heart," but the reasons aren't always as evident as they are for the psalmist. What contrast did he make about the contents of his heart? (See verses 2 and 5.)

In this last section, the psalmist's mindset appears to change as he expresses new confidence. When we are in grief, we need somewhere to place our trust and hope, even when we don't feel like it. This is an important transition from lament to trust and praise of God.

Although the psalmist ends in praise, his questions remain unanswered. The lament doesn't have the happy ending we hope for, with a dramatic portrayal of deliverance where God appears on the scene and rights all the wrongs. Yet in the height of the story's hopeless tension, we get a different happy ending: the psalmist makes an abrupt turn with an expression of confidence. He chooses to trust in God's eventual action and rest in the hope of deliverance. He doesn't lose his faith in Yahweh's mercy, kindness, and goodness. We see a dynamic tension between lament and praise, an inner struggle between humanity and God. And in the end, this psalm rests in the unfailing character of God.

Take some time to reflect on the psalm you've just examined and form a clearer determination of your own current views of God. Be as specific as possible with your answers because it may be helpful to return to this section in a few months to see what progress you've made.

> I see God as…

> My views of God most recently changed because…

A Do-It-Yourself Lament

Now that you've examined someone else's psalm of lament, I challenge you to write one of your own. I think a lament is appropriate, because I have discovered that one thing all healthy grievers have in common is the ability to be real. When they are feeling sorrow, anger, frustration, or doubt, they can own those emotions and be okay with them. Yet they are still able to perceive those raw emotions within a larger context and appeal to God for assistance and strength. They actively work to realign their thoughts toward surrender and willingness to place their trust in God.

So, following the format of Psalm 13, follow these steps to write your personal psalm of lament.

> **Step 1**: First, choose an appropriate name for God. Psalm 13 addressed God as *Yahweh* (Almighty God), but God—who includes Jesus and the Holy Spirit—has many names and titles. Select one that is meaningful to you: Father? Creator? Great Physician? Teacher? Advocate? Counselor? Etc.

Step 2: Next, tell God your grievance and how you are feeling about it. As you have seen, you can (and should) be completely honest. You may use singular pronouns ("I" and "me") and make it very personal. Or if you know others who are suffering in the same way, you can write on behalf of your community of grievers, using "we").

Step 3: Describe what you would like God to do, and why.

Step 4: What truth about God can you affirm, even in your grief, to demonstrate your faith that he will hear and act?

Step 5: Offer God whatever praise you can in your current state of mind. If nothing else, thank him for hearing your lament.

Your Lament

Don't be troubled if you can't complete all the steps. During early stages of grief, you may only be able to get through the first three steps. It might be months or years before you're truly ready for the fourth and fifth steps. And as you move into the fourth step, you may first have to write at a cognitive level that you don't yet feel in your heart. However, it's amazing how frequently this act of faith is like a self-fulfilling prophecy. You first write what you believe to be true, and surprise, you begin to experience that truth in your life.

After you've written your lament psalm, I encourage you to share it with at least one other person. If you share with someone else who is grieving, challenge him or her to complete this exercise as well. And if you're in a small group, it can be powerful for each person to write a lament and then read it to the group. As you minister to others in this way, it will minister to you as well.

Keep a copy of your lament somewhere you will see it occasionally. Hopefully, months or years from now it will be a reminder of dark days that are now long behind you and how far you've come since then.

What Next?

If you're currently in a season of grief, the lament psalms can be a great consolation to you. You need to be assured that everyone goes through those seasons, and aware that most people keep moving forward until they're able to feel joy and peace again. So I want to leave you with one last assignment. You may not be ready for it yet, but as soon as you think you are, I urge you to try it. First, take a look at Psalms 146—150. These are a series of praise psalms, with each one opening and closing with the phrase "Praise the Lord" (literally, "Hallelujah!"). See how it's done, and then try to write your own praise psalm, just as you did your psalm of lament.

I still want you to be absolutely honest with God. If you're not able to genuinely praise him for anything yet, then don't. I'm not advising you to "fake it till you make it." I don't believe God wants us to fake *anything* with him. But I *am* asking you to consider if you can't come up with something you can praise him for. Did the sun come up again this morning? Do you have anyone who loves you and cares about you? Are you able to see and hear, taste and smell? (Even if you have no desire for music or appetite for food at this point, isn't it good to know your body will ready when your emotions are?) The more you connect with God through praise, the less of a hold grief will have on you.

Almost 20 years ago, I met Robert Rogers after his wife and four children died in a tragic flash flood incident that washed their car off the interstate and over an embankment. I got involved when a friend who was working as a grief counselor at the funeral home asked for my help. She said Robert wasn't grieving like people expected him to grieve. He seemed to be "doing too well," in their words. He was strong in his faith, which many people interpreted as denial. I kept up with him for the next ten years as he left a career in engineering to go into ministry.

What I found most fascinating about Robert was that he hardly bothered with the usual "Why?" questions. When I asked him if he had ever questioned God, he said that had at first, but that he felt it was more important to focus on "What now?" He believed that God had allowed him to go through this tragedy for a reason, so he wanted to find out what he was supposed to do in the aftermath.

Robert started speaking at churches, encouraging people with a powerful message to "Live a Life of No Regrets." Through his ministry, Mighty in the Land, he has encouraged thousands of people during their losses and crisis situations, offering hope. His faith in God has not only enabled him to survive, but to rebuild his life. He remarried, and it has been a joy to watch God bless him with a new family—a beautiful wife and children. God has been faithful to guide and sustain him through unbelievable loss.

Robert chose to put his faith and trust in God when it seemed that all was lost. I share his story frequently, in hopes that others (and now you) will do the same.

When Joshua was about to lead the Israelites into the Promised Land, God told him three times: "Be strong and courageous" (Joshua 1:6, 7, 9). Joshua still needed to get the people across the Jordan River at flood stage (which he did just as Moses had taken them through the Red Sea— on dry land [Joshua 3—4]). He was yet to fight the Battle of Jericho (Joshua 6). But he faithfully kept moving forward until the Israelites were, at long last, in the land that God had promised Abraham centuries before.

You will certainly face your own floods of doubt and battles of the mind as you deal with grief, but the strategy is the same: Keep moving forward. Don't give up. God has a wonderful plan for you. One of my favorite Scriptures that I remind people of in the darkest days of their grief is Jeremiah 19:11: "'For I know the plans I have for you,' declares the LORD, 'plans to prosper you and not to harm you, plans to give you hope and a future.'"

I hope your future looks a bit brighter now than it did as you began this workbook. Grief can harden or soften you. It can slow you down and turn you inward for examination while at the same time turning you outward and showing your inadequacy to do life alone. We need both the power of God and the support of community if we are going to not only survive loss but grow through it.

It is my prayer that you will invite the amazing God who loves you into your life in an intimate way and surrender to his full lordship of your life. That's what the most healthy grievers do. I pray that God uses your current grief to shape you into a person of greater sensitivity and compassion for others, willing and eager to comfort them with the comfort you receive from God. He can surely do it. Just be strong and courageous.

Final Exercise: Grief and Your Expanding World

I have one final exercise for you. People often ask me, "When will this pain end? How long will my grief last?" I know it's painful . . . and at times seems unbearable. Early in the book I talked about things changing in frequency, intensity, and duration. When people ask me about the end of their grief, I often draw a circle on the left side of a piece of paper. I say, "This circle represents your life." I hand them a pen and explain, "Fill in the circle with the amount of space your grief takes up today." And now I'm asking you to do the same thing.

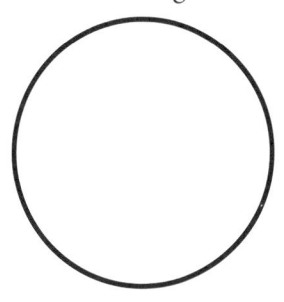

Sometimes the grief can feel so overwhelming that it dominates 98 percent of your world—illustrated in the early grief phase. Here is the analogy I share with people: If you were trapped in a room that was totally dark, there were no windows, and you wanted to get the darkness out, what could you do? Can you push the darkness out? Can you vacuum out the darkness? No, the only way to get darkness out of a room is to introduce light. How would you do that? You might say, "I could turn on a light." But the power is out, so that doesn't work. You could light a candle, but the lighter is out of fluid. You try to use the flashlight on your phone, but it's out of power. Every attempt ends in failure. But there's another option: If you don't want to be in the dark, you can open the door, leave the room, and walk into a space that's full of light. It seems like a very simple and workable solution, but many people aren't willing to take this step. Their darkened room has become a familiar place—it's all they now know—so stepping into another space is terrifying.

This is the challenge of grief. If you're going to be a healthy griever at some point after you have sat in the darkness of your lament, you have to get up and step into a world that will seem very different than your loss. You may feel alone in your journey even though you have others around you. You can take some steps of your grief journey with others, but you must take some steps alone. This is one of them.

Healthy grievers allow themselves to experience the painful emotions of their grief, but sooner or later, they also step into places they once went and new places they haven't ever gone. They add new rings of expanding experience to their world, as illustrated in this example. As you add new dimensions to your world, your grief will shrink in relation to the rest of your life.

Think about one thing you can do right now that will help dispel some of your grief's darkness. It can be calling a friend, engaging in a hobby, spending time in nature, enjoying a pet, volunteering to serve, listening to an encouraging podcast, or pointing your heart toward God in worship. It's different for each person, so you need to find whatever works for you. But if you want your grief to shrink, you can't just try to push your grief out of your world. The harder you try not to grieve, the more it will dominate your life and "come out sideways." Step into your grief, experience your sorrow, and allow yourself to mourn your loss. Sit in the seat of suffering as long as you need to, but there will be a time to move forward, even though it feels awkward, painful, confusing, and even wrong. God will be with you in this journey if you invite Him to be with you. Finding the courage to step into the light doesn't mean your grief is over. You will grieve elements of your loss for the rest of your life. It's about choosing to experience new life and joy in the midst of your sorrow so that gradually, your life is no longer consumed with grief.

Reflection Exercise

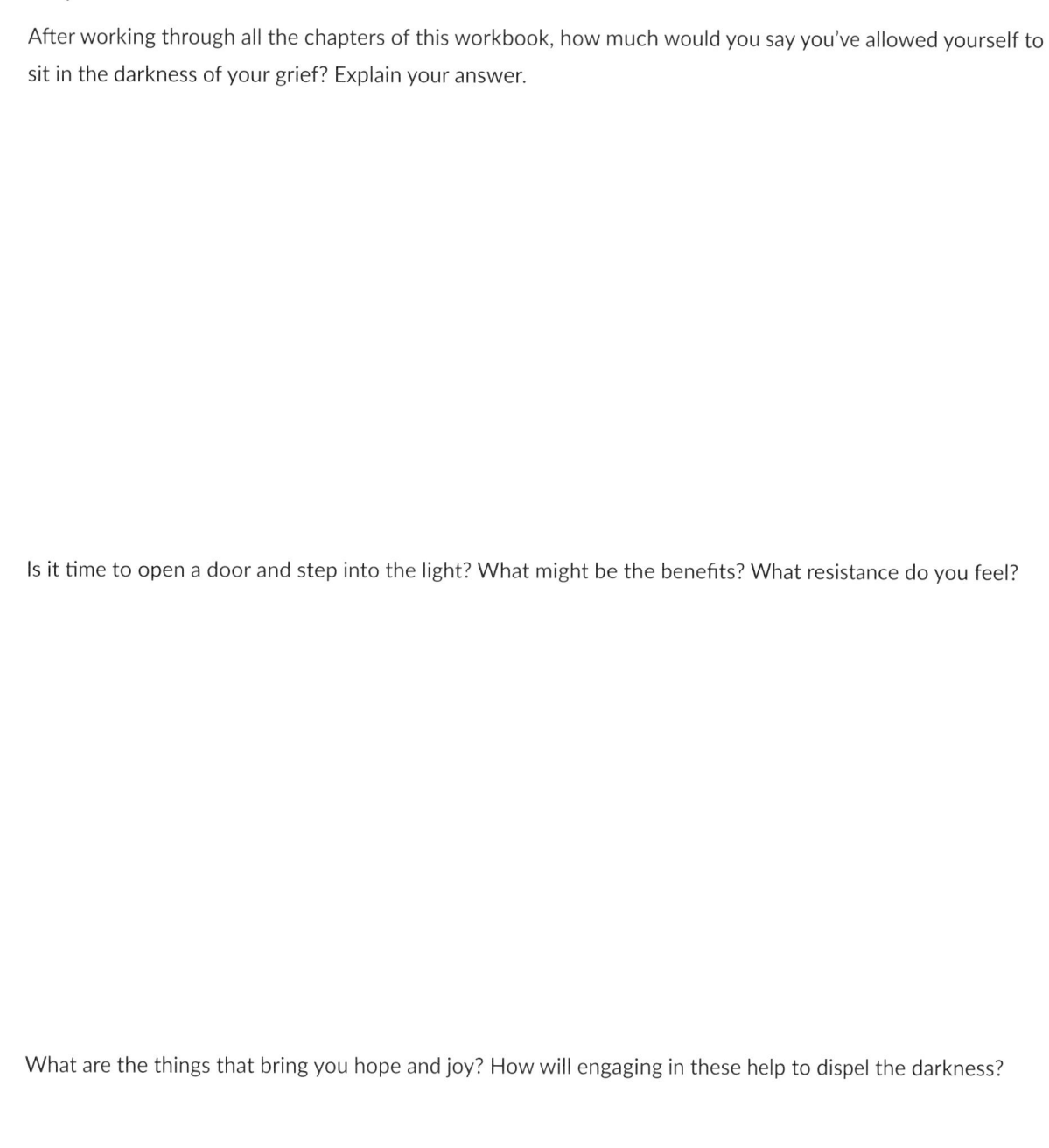

After working through all the chapters of this workbook, how much would you say you've allowed yourself to sit in the darkness of your grief? Explain your answer.

Is it time to open a door and step into the light? What might be the benefits? What resistance do you feel?

What are the things that bring you hope and joy? How will engaging in these help to dispel the darkness?

Now, at the end of the workbook, many people benefit by going through it again. This time, they gain more insights, find more courage, and make more progress. What's your next step?

I would like to close by reflecting on a wonderful quote from Elisabeth Kubler-Ross, one I have used in my grief classes for many years. It is my prayer that God will be present with you in your grief, and He will use the refinement process of experiencing your pain to make you a more beautiful person.

> The beautiful people are those who have known defeat, known suffering, known struggle, known loss, and have found their way out of the depths. These people have appreciation, and sensitivity, and an understanding of life that fills them with compassion, gentleness, and a deep, loving concern. Beautiful people do not just happen.[16]

APPENDIX

Bible Passages for Those Who Grieve

Scriptures for Comfort

Matthew 11: 28-30

Come to me, all of you who are weary and carry heavy burdens, and I will give you rest. Take my yoke upon you. Let me teach you, because I am humble and gentle at heart, and you will find rest for your souls. For my yoke is easy to bear, and the burden I give you is light.

2 Corinthians 1:3-4

All praise to God, the Father of our Lord Jesus Christ. God is our merciful Father and the source of all comfort. He comforts us in all our troubles so that we can comfort others. When they are troubled, we will be able to give them the same comfort God has given us.

Psalm 23

The Lord is my shepherd; I have all that I need. He lets me rest in green meadows; leads me beside peaceful streams. He renews my strength. He guides me along right paths, bringing honor to his name. Even when I walk through the darkest valley, I will not be afraid, for you are close beside me. Your rod and your staff protect and comfort me. You prepare a feast for me in the presence of my enemies. You honor me by anointing my head with oil. My cup overflows with blessings. Surely your goodness and unfailing love will pursue me all the days of my life and I will live in the house of the Lord forever.

Matthew 5:4

Blessed are those who mourn, for they will be comforted.

Psalm 34:18

The Lord is close to the brokenhearted; he rescues those whose spirits are crushed.

Lamentations 3:22-26, 31-33

The faithful love of the Lord never ends! His mercies never cease. Great is his faithfulness; his mercies begin afresh each morning. I say to myself, "The Lord is my inheritance; therefore, I will hope in him! The Lord is good to those who depend on him, to those who search for him. So it is good to wait quietly for salvation from the Lord. For no one is abandoned by the Lord forever. Though he brings grief, he also shows compassion because of the greatness of his unfailing love. For he does not enjoy hurting people or causing them sorrow.

God's Promises In Your Sorrow

John 14:1-3

Don't let your hearts be troubled. Trust in God, and trust also in me. There is more than enough room in my Father's home. If this were not so, would I have told you that I am going to prepare a place for you? When everything is ready, I will come and get you, so that you will always be with me where I am.

Romans 8:35, 37-39

Can anything ever separate us from Christ's love? Does it mean he no longer loves us if we have trouble or calamity, or are persecuted, or hungry, or destitute, or in danger, or threatened with death? No, despite all these things, overwhelming victory is ours through Christ, who loved us. And I am convinced that nothing can ever separate us from God's love. Neither death nor life, neither angels nor demons, neither our fears for today nor our worries about tomorrow—not even the powers of hell can separate us from God's love. No power in the sky above or in the earth below—indeed, nothing in all creation will ever be able to separate us from the love of God that is revealed in Christ Jesus our Lord.

Isaiah 41:10

So do not fear, for I am with you; do not be dismayed, for I am your God. I will strengthen you and help you; I will uphold you with my righteous right hand.

John 14:27

I am leaving you with a gift—peace of mind and heart. And the peace I give is a gift the world cannot give. So don't be troubled or afraid.

Psalm 56:10-13

I praise God for what he has promised; yes, I praise the Lord for what he has promised. I trust in God, so why should I be afraid? What can mere mortals do to me? I will fulfill my vows to you, O God, and will offer a sacrifice of thanks for your help. For you have rescued me from death; you have kept my feet from slipping. So now I can walk in your presence, O God, in your life-giving light.

Hope for the Future

1 Corinthians 15:50-57

What I am saying, dear brothers and sisters, is that our physical bodies cannot inherit the Kingdom of God. These dying bodies cannot inherit what will last forever. But let me reveal to you a wonderful secret. We will not all die, but we will all be transformed! It will happen in a moment, in the blink of an eye, when the last trumpet is blown. For when the trumpet sounds, those who have died will be raised to live forever. And we who are living will also be transformed. For our dying bodies must be transformed into bodies that will never die; our mortal bodies must be transformed into immortal bodies. Then, when our dying bodies have been transformed into bodies that will never die, this Scripture will be fulfilled: "Death is swallowed up in victory. O death, where is your victory? O death, where is your sting?" For sin is the sting that results in death, and the law gives sin its power. But thank God! He gives us victory over sin and death through our Lord Jesus Christ.

John 11:25-26

Jesus told her, "I am the resurrection and the life. Anyone who believes in me will live, even after dying. Everyone who lives in me and believes in me will never ever die.

Job 19:25-27

But as for me, I know that my Redeemer lives, and he will stand upon the earth at last. And after my body has decayed, yet in my body I will see God! I will see him for myself. Yes, I will see him with my own eyes. I am overwhelmed at the thought!

Philippians 1:21-23

For to me, living means living for Christ, and dying is even better. But if I live, I can do more fruitful work for Christ. So I really don't know which is better I'm torn between two desires: I long to go and be with Christ, which would be far better for me.

Endnotes

1. Kevin Ellers, *The Grief Factor* (Crystal Lake, IL: ICC Publishing, 2023).

2. C. S. Lewis, *The Four Loves* (New York: Houghton Mifflin Harcourt, 1991), p. 121.

3. Dietrich Bonhoeffer, *Letters and Papers from Prison (Vol. 8)* (Fortress Press, 2010), p. 176.

4. Kenneth J. Doka and Terry L. Martin, *Men Don't Cry, Women Do: Transcending Gender Stereotypes of Grief* (New York: Routledge, 1999) and *Grieving Beyond Gender: Understanding the Ways Men and Women Mourn* (New York: Routledge, 2010).

5. Vivek Murthy, "Our Epidemic of Loneliness and Isolation: The U.S. Surgeon General's Advisory on the Healing Effects of Social Connection and Community," Office of the U.S. Surgeon General, 2023.

6. J.C. Badcock, J. Holt-Lunstad, P. Bombaci, E. Garcia, and M.H. Lim, *Position Statement: Addressing Social Isolation and Loneliness and the Power of Human Connection*, Global Initiative on Loneliness and Connection (GICL), 2002 and J. Holt-Lunstad, "Why Social Relationships Are Important for Physical Health: A Systems Approach to Understanding and Modifying Risk and Protection," *Annual Review of Psychology* 2018; 69:437-458.

7. Robert Browning Hamilton, "Along the Road," *Sage Journals*, Volume 1, Issue 3, https://doi.org/10.1177/002205741508100

8. T.A. Rando, *Treatment of Complicated Mourning* (Champaign, IL: Research Press, 1993).

9. Jeremy Holmes, *John Bowlby and Attachment Theory* (New York: Routledge, 2014).

10. C. S. Lewis, *Grief Observed* (Grand Rapids: Zondervan, 2001), p. 51.

11. Rando, ibid.

12. Source Center for Action & Contemplation: https://cac.org/: *Daily insights from Fr Rohr and the CAC.*

13. K.L. Ellers, *The Grief Factor* (Crystal Lake, IL: ICC Publishing, 2003).

14. C.S. Lewis, *A Grief Observed* (New York: HarperSanFrancisco, 1961, 2001), pp. 3, 5-7.

15. G. H. Wilson, *Psalms, Volume 1, The NIV Application Commentary*, Gen. Ed. Terry Muck (Grand Rapids, MI: Zondervan, 2002).

16. Walter Brueggemann, *The Message of the Psalms* (Minneapolis: Augsburg, 1984).

17. Elisabeth Kubler-Ross, *Death: The Final Stage of Growth* (Hoboken, N.J.: Prentice-Hall, 1975).

About the Author

Kevin Ellers, D.Min., currently serves as the Territorial Disaster Services and Chaplaincy Director for The Salvation Army in the U.S.A. Central Territory and has been with this organization for over 28 years. As President and Founder of the Institute for Compassionate Care and RESET Life Coaching, he finds great fulfillment working along with his wife Jennifer as they partner with horses for equine-assisted coaching. His passion is to coach people through crisis, grief, and workplace difficulties, as well as serving as an executive coach in leadership development. He feels honored to walk alongside people in their journey to achieve higher levels of personal and professional growth and healing.

His love for curriculum development and training is fulfilled in teaching through The Salvation Army and serving as faculty for the International Critical Incident Stress Foundation. He also served as an adjunct professor at Olivet Nazarene University, teaching in the areas of crisis response and chaplaincy. As an author and speaker, this passion has opened many doors to teach broadly to diverse groups in the areas of grief, trauma, disasters, resilience, and emotional and spiritual wellness.

Ellers has authored or co-authored the following: *The First 48 Hours: Spiritual Caregivers as First Responders*; *Grief Following Trauma*; *The Grief Factor*; *Emotional and Spiritual Care in Disasters*; *Spiritual and Psychological First Aid*; *Understanding Suicide: Effective Tools for Prevention*; and *Stress, Compassion Fatigue and Resiliency*.

For the past 30 years, Ellers has provided direct care and critical incident stress management and crisis leadership in large-scale trauma events like 9/11 at the World Trade Center and Hurricane Katrina to countless critical incidents, including suicides, homicides, mass shootings, assaults, and chronic illnesses. He also has a passion for helping emergency responders and serves as a lead chaplain with the Illinois State Fraternal Order of Police.

Join the world's leading faith-based counseling organization today!

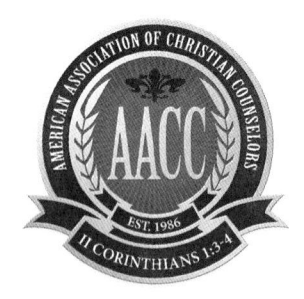

American Association *of* Christian Counselors

Building Excellence & Professionalism in Christian Counseling

Presidential Member Benefits

- *Christian Counseling Today* Magazine
  AACC's quarterly, award-winning magazine

- *Christian Counseling Connection* Newsletter
  Quarterly, cutting-edge newsletter

- Christian Care Connect
  One Year Membership

- CounselBytes
  Bi-monthly audio interviews featuring relevant topics in Christian counseling

- AACC eNews
  Monthly electronic journal

- Clinical Insights
  Monthly, your questions answered by leading professionals

- CounselTrends
  Monthly video with leading professionals

- Counseltalk Webinars
  Monthly video-based online Webinars

- Discounts on Conferences and Educational Resources

- Certificate of Membership
  Suitable for framing

- *AND MORE!*

christianCAREconnect
connecting clients, counselors, coaches & clinics

Presidential Membership
New Members Only $79
(REGULAR DUES $189 — RENEWAL $89/YEAR)

Growing Stronger Every Day!

1.800.526.8673 • AACC.net

MHC FR

CERTIFIED
Mental Health Coach
FIRST RESPONDER TRAINING

Become a Mental Health Coach! Over 15,000 churches and 30,000 students enrolled!

LIMITED TIME SCHOLARSHIP
No cost to the church and tuition is FREE for students!
(One-time $54 tech support fee applies)

"Without question, this training will be one of the most, if not the most, significant projects we have ever done in the history of the AACC. We need an army of helpers in the local church—those of whom God has given natural gifts and talents to offer help, hope, and guidance to the hurting!"

Dr. Tim Clinton, President
American Association of Christian Counselors

Introducing the Mental Health Coach Training, a 42-hour, biblically-based training that consists of three courses. Enroll and successfully complete all three courses and become a **"Certified Mental Health Coach"** by the International Board of Christian Care.

Our 2023 mission is to engage, educate and equip an additional 6,500 churches and congregations and to train 45,000 students all over America and around the world.

Who can enroll? Under the discretion of your church, **anyone with a calling to offer help, hope, and encouragement** to those who are hurting and looking for guidance and direction in everyday life.

- 42-hour, Biblically-based, clinically-excellent training program
- Featuring some of the world's leading mental health and ministry experts
- Study anywhere, anytime, at your own pace, on any of your favorite devices!
- On-demand video lectures—No schedules!
- Available 24/7/365
- And you have one year to complete your course

Learn to help those who struggle with **Serious Mental Illness (SMI),** including topics like:

- Addiction
- Trauma and Abuse
- Grief and Loss
- Boundaries
- Panic Disorders
- PTSD
- Phobias
- Suicide
- Crisis Intervention
- Depression
- Stress and Anxiety
  ... and more!

LIGHTUNIVERSITY.COM/MENTALHEALTHCOACH

CONTINUING EDUCATION AND ONLINE CERTIFICATION FOR COUNSELING PROFESSIONALS

LIGHT UNIVERSITY

A Global Leader in Certificate and Diploma-Based Education

The Leader in Certificate and Diploma Based Christian Counseling Education

5 SCHOOLS OF STUDY & OVER **200 COURSES** TO CHOOSE FROM!

BIBLICAL COUNSELING
Gain crucial knowledge necessary to help others with confidence using the Bible and the latest counseling wisdom and insights.

LIFE COACHING
Make a difference in the lives of your clients by integrating sound biblical principles with relevant life coaching materials and professional practice.

CRISIS RESPONSE
Provide immediate assitance to emergency and disaster relief agencies with effective Christian leadership and biblically-based principles.

MARRIAGE AND FAMILY
Help clients preserve and promote the institution of marriage, family and the biblical principles on which they are based.

MENTAL HEALTH COACHING
Help clients obtain and maintain stability, manage difficult symptoms, rebuild relationships, and find a purpose for living.

CONTINUING EDUCATION
Browse our extensive course catalog for continuing education credits of your professional counseling license.

Visit the **all-new LightUniversity.com** website, featuring **new and improved search capabilities, course bundling options,** and more!

1-800-526-8673 • ADMISSIONS@LIGHTUNIVERSITY.COM

6-Week Introductory Study of Biblical Counseling

COFFEE CUP COUNSELING
training program

Anger, Depression, Stress, Loss, Betrayal...

"WHAT TO SAY WHEN YOU DON'T KNOW WHAT TO SAY; WHAT TO DO WHEN YOU DON'T KNOW WHAT TO DO."

Lessons Include:
Week 1: Caring for People in Need
- Tim Clinton, Ed.D.
Week 2: Models of Care
- Ron Hawkins, D.Min., Ed.D.
Week 3: Becoming a Great Listener
- Mercy Connors, Ph.D.
Week 4: Relying on the Scriptures and Prayer
- Ron Hawkins, D.Min., Ed.D.
Week 5: Resources and Referrals
- Mercy Connors, Ph.D.
Week 6: Getting Started
- Tim Clinton, Ed.D.

In the six weeks of training, you'll learn:
- The privilege and responsibility of stepping into people's lives when they're most vulnerable
- The biblical basis of caring friendships
- A time-tested, three-step model of helping
- How to care for people in times of crisis
- How to become a skilled and effective listener
- How to address the difficult issues of abuse and boundaries
- How to establish a network of competent professionals for referrals
- And many other insights and practical skills you can use!

1-800-526-8673 • AACC.NET

Resources

MORE WORKBOOKS IN THIS SERIES

THE CHRISTIAN COUNSELING WORKBOOK SERIES
A Guide to Help Overcome Life's Challenging Moments

HOPE & HEALING FOR DEPRESSION

GREGORY L. JANTZ, PH.D
with KEITH WALL

THE CHRISTIAN COUNSELING WORKBOOK SERIES
A Guide to Holistic Recovery

HOPE & HEALING FOR FOOD ADDICTION

WRITTEN BY
RHONA EPSTEIN, PSY.D

THE CHRISTIAN COUNSELING WORKBOOK SERIES
A Guide to Help Flourish in Community

HOPE & HEALING FOR LONELINESS

WRITTEN BY
MARK MAYFIELD, PH.D

THE CHRISTIAN COUNSELING WORKBOOK SERIES
A Guide to Healing Through Loss

HOPE & HEALING FOR GRIEF

WRITTEN BY
KEVIN ELLERS, D. MIN.

To order these workbooks, go to www.aacc.net